I0767100

In the Beast's Alley
(Poems of conscience)

Tontongi

Trilingual Press: PO Box 391206, Cambridge, MA 02139
E-mail: trilingualpress@tanbou.com
Tel. 617-331-2269

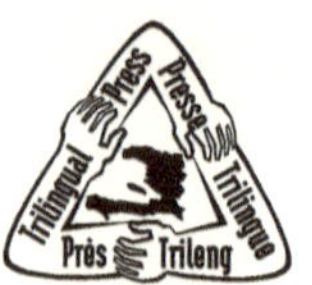

Graphic design: David Henry, www.davidphenry.com

Photos and front cover concept: Patrick Sylvain
ISBN 13: 978-1-936431-13-7
ISBN 10: 1-936431-13-0

Library of Congress Control Number: 2013940760
Printed in the United States of America
First edition: October 2013

In the Beast's Alley
(Poems of conscience)

Tontongi

Trilingual Press, Boston, Massachusetts

Other books by the same author;
Lòt liv pibliye pa menm otè a;
Autres livres du même auteur:

Poetica Agwe, poems and essays in Haitian, French, and English (Trilingual Press, Boston 2011).

Critique de la francophonie haïtienne (essais en français et en haïtien, éd. l'Harmattan, Paris 2007).

The Vodou Gods' Joy/Rejwisans lwa yo (epic, bilingual poems English-Ayisyen, ed. Tambour, Boston 1997).

The Dream of Being (poems in English co-authored with Gary Hicks; ed. New Strategy Book, Boston 1991).

La présidence d'Aristide : Entre le défi et l'espoir (français et ayisyen, éd. New Strategy Books, Boston 1990).

Cri de rêve (poèmes en français et en ayisyen, éd. New Strategy Book, Boston 1986).

Books edited or co-edited by the author / Liv ki edite oubyen ko-edite pa otè a / Ouvrages édités ou co-édités par l'auteur:

The Anthology of Liberation Poetry, English poems co-edited with Jill Netchinsky (TP, Boston 2012).

Voices of the Sun: The Anthology of Haitian Writers Published in the Review Tanbou / Vwa Solèy pale : Antoloji ekriven ayisyen ki pibliye nan revi Tanbou / Les Voix du Soleil : Anthologie des écrivains haïtiens publiés dans la revue Tanbou (TP, Boston 2009).

Poets Against the Killing Fields, poems in English (TP, Boston 2007).

 In the Beast's Alley (Poems of conscience)

Acknowledgments

Poetry can join with politics, that is collective practical action, to force equity against the egoism of a minority that perverts life's equilibrium. Having spent now more than half of my life in the United States, I grow to love the American people whom I find very open to the progressive dynamic of History, even if they do allow themselves all too often to be zombified by the marvelous attraction of materialistic capitalism and nihilism promoted by official and mass-media propaganda.

I extend thanks to the following friends, fellow poets and thinkers: the Laraque brothers, Paul and Franck, Denizé Lauture, Berthony Dupont, Aldo Tambellini, Brenda Walcott, Idi Jawarakim, Gary Hicks, Jack Hirschman, Askia Touré, Anna Wexler, Charlot Lucien, Doumafis Lafontant, Frantz-Antoine Leconte, Everett Hoagland, Patrick Sylvain, Danielle Legros-Georges, and others with whom I have been lucky to exchange poetic thoughts and who share the notion of poetry as not only cosmic effusion and aesthetic decoration, but also as socio-existential engagement and critical conscience.

Many thanks to the following persons for helping in the production of this book:

Patrick Sylvain, for providing the cover concept, and for taking the time to photograph the Boston South End streets which I referred to in my poem "I see coming the ghost," his photos add a special dimension to the book; my wife Jill Netchinsky, fellow poet and Latin American scholar, for helping with the editing of the prose and who tolerates my stylistic idiosyncrasies and stubbornness;

David Henry for invaluable help with graphic design and for being a supportive asset for all these years; all my family members, friends and acquaintances who have contributed to the fermentation of the ideas, emotions and thoughts articulated in this collection. You all have my gratitude. The struggle for a qualitative and humanist life continues.

—*Tontongi*, June 2013

Some of the poems in this collection were previously published in my trilingual book *Poetica Agwe*, and in the anthologies *Liberation Poetry*, *Poets Against the Killing Fields*, *The Anthology of Haitian Poets in Massachusetts*, and in the publications *Street Magazine*, *Haïti-Progrès*, *Auscultations*, and *Tanbou*. Most of the poems, however, have never been published before, appearing here for the first time. I hope you, the reader, enjoy this trans-temporal foray into my poetry of conscience.

Table of Contents

                                                         In the Beast's Alley (Poems of conscience)

In the Beast's Alley (Poems of conscience)

Introduction

My poems show human beings for what they are: both evil and capable of transcendence. My poems, while militant in their revolutionary spirit, also reflect the belief that a world of tolerance and shared love is possible. My poems express the need for peace as a space that cultivates solidarity and empathy with others. Peace is a political process, because one makes peace with his or her harmful enemies, not with harmless friends—especially when we know that representations of the enemy are for the most part false, based on prejudices (sometimes on purely subjective presuppositions), or on objective interests.

The first part of this collection is entitled "The Gaze of the Other: Testimony and Observance" to underline their use as reverse-anthropological testimony from a gaze—the gaze of the Other—that is not always noticed. The present collection, in line with my previous book *Poetica Agwe*, continues the reflection on this other conscience while reviving the memory of my sojourn in the West—France and United States. The beast's alley is a metaphor for my living in the struggling part of these lands.

The second part, "Power and Tribulations," addresses issues of war and domination. Since the poet lives in a particular time and age, my poetry is also a reflection of the concerns of the historical time in which I live. Victor Hugo's genius is informed by the socio-economic conditions of nineteenth-century France, including the Parisian Revolution of 1848 and the reign of Napoleon III. My poetry is informed by the nefarious Duvalierist regimes, the trauma of displacement and exile, the witnessing of horrors in *my* world, such as the South African apartheid regime, the Israeli occupation of Palestine, the anti-insurgency repressions in Latin America, the Iraq and Afghanistan wars. These constitute the backdrop against which my consciousness has taken form and evolved.

The third part of this book, "New Poems and New Horizons," contains the most recently written poems and casts light on the universality of evil and on the entrenchment of ideological and socio-economic interests. Like my poems on the January 2010 Haitian earthquake, the two poems here dedicated to the 2013 Boston Marathon victims express a deep sorrow from a tragedy that hit home in a personal way. The poem "Boston's Gripping Charm" proposes that the violence of human action, even when attributable to rational, reasonable and even legitimate grievances, is a repudiation of the ideal of human togetherness and peace which we should all thrive to implement. At the same time, it is not my role to tell oppressed people how to resist their oppression, especially when their friends and families are being slaughtered by powerful invading armies.

Ultimately, the poem expresses satisfaction that despite the suffering, *"still the horror could not kill the people's / marvelous union and communal aim to stay put, / strong Boston remains even in pain."*

Despite the fact that violence often serves the interests of the belligerents, in the last analysis, violence brings nothing of value to the moral finality of human problematics. As Fanon and Sartre have said, the counter-violence of the oppressed restores their humanity in a situation of totalitarian violence that dehumanizes them, but the

                    In the Beast's Alley (Poems of conscience)

realization of being implies an ethical and paradigmatic overtaking of, together, the savagery of physical crude force, the coercion of economic imperatives and the zombification of intellectual assumptions.

I write almost equally in English, in French and in Haitian Creole; this is my second collection of poems written entirely in English. The first was *The Dream of Being* (1992), co-written with African-American poet Gary Hicks. It took me a while to decide to write in English; I resisted it until I discovered it is one of the most beautiful languages in the world. Like Haitian Creole, it is malleable to play, to experimentation, to daring creation.

I approach my writing in the English language as I do the preparation of a meal: I use the ingredients at my disposal to create an entirely new product. A product both familiar and out of the ordinary, delicious and doubtful, appetizing and indiscernible. Writing in a language I learned by necessity compelled me to create a new language, my language, the product of my *entendement*, of my own mind.

To the extent that language expresses our inner thoughts and experience, it is also testimony, the expression of memory. When it expresses hope and future projection, it embodies a means for change.

This book is in part about my connection to the US people, to the land, to the culture. I claim affiliation with the anti-monarchist rebels like Tom Paine and the antislavery insurgents like Harriet Tubman, John Brown and Frederick Douglass who honored by their deeds and praxis the humanist values of freedom and social justice. As a country of immigrants, the United States internalizes the many conflicts and tensions that the displaced—yes, in fact, the immigrants are *displaced*—bring to their new refuge. Being part of this maelstrom of fantasy and dream is a great privilege of my life.

I also identify with the indigenous peoples who, like the anti-colonialists Caonabo and Anacaona in Haiti, resisted the trampling of their rights by the newcomers. They paid the genocidal price as a result. Giants like Toussaint, Dessalines, Bolívar, Marti, and Castro, Chavez, would continue the tradition of resistance.

My poems are expressions of my conscience and my affect, my state of being and feeling. They are as well *testimony* as far as they memorialize instants of the passing time. My poetry is a cry of conscience, an appeal to surpass bad faith, a reach to transcendence.

Finally, my poems want to reaffirm the notion that we are companions in the adventure of life, brothers, sisters, comrades, and fellow-travelers on life's journey. We are not natural enemies but, to the contrary, allies ineluctably bound in the great project of realization of a human society which supports a universal justice system that defends the rights of all and of each one of us. A society which preserves the qualitative integrity of a safe and livable ecologic environment, and which honors national self-determination for all; a society liberated from the mercantilist imperatives of capitalist corporations. A society liberated from hatred, exclusion, and exploitation of others. A society that reaches humanity.

The alley of the beast has not only produced oppressive and deceptive outcomes: it is also a source for learning the many dimensions of reality, including the

In the Beast's Alley (Poems of conscience)

relativity of defeat and victory, dismissal and glory, loss and enrichment.

These poems of conscience are poems of love, because love is the active part of conscience, the effort toward the realization of what is both just and beautiful.

—*Tontongi*, May 2013

In the Beast's Alley (Poems of conscience)

The Nexus of Poetry and Photography

—by Patrick Sylvain

I am a loaded camera with an open shutter, sensitive to movement and light. I frame my world inside other frames, at times with words and at other times with film. I'm an active zoom, capturing a stick landing body blows, or an aged rouged mouth scatting into a silver microphone. Whatever goes into my darkroom mind must at one point be developed. A picture, a poem, the world is my subject as I am subject to it.

All Ideas and memories cannot jump at once onto the page, a filtering process must first occur. Likewise for photography, although all subjects can be interesting not all subjects at all times can be captivating. One must isolate the secondary and tertiary subjects in order to bring into focus, or attention, the primary subject. Your view becomes a truth in that vast array of point of views and vantage points. However, one must learn to be critical of the viewpoints, the angles, the words, the metaphors, the contents and contexts of one's work.

Whether poetry or photography, study the masters, learn their techniques, be critical of their shortcomings, try to reproduce their best-loved work and then detach yourself from them in order to ascend your own voice, your own technique. Just as in photography where one should get in close to subject, the poem should also be close and personal; it should fill the frame so to speak…

I am a loaded camera and with my reflective eye-lenses, I search for peculiarities, quaint angles, converging idiosyncrasies and buoyant lights that awake the senses.

I do my best to obey my internal meter while paying
attention to line breaks. A line must never be neglected.
There are essential details in lines. Even a broken line, an
odd angle, carries valuable details and history…

I photograph with the poet's sense of a perfect com-
position and cadence, but I write with the photographer's
awareness of time, depth, dimension and frame.

—*Patrick Sylvain,* teacher, writer, photographer, 2013

          In the Beast's Alley (Poems of conscience)

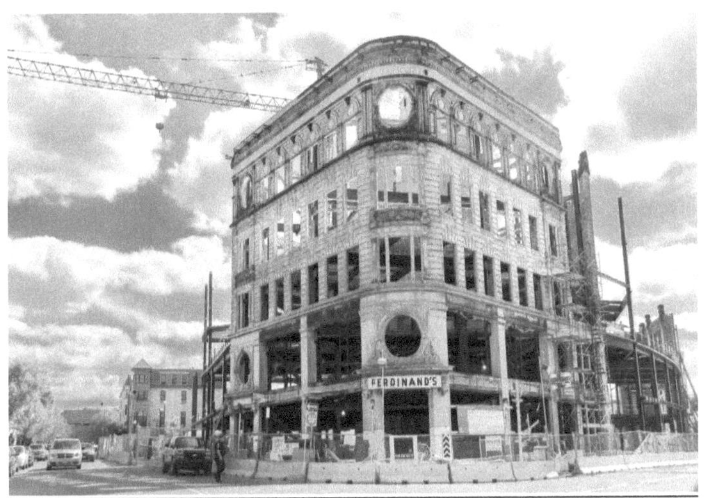

The modernization of the Ferdinand Building in Dudley Square, Roxbury —*photo by Patrick Sylvain, 2013.*

In the Beast's Alley (Poems of conscience)

Part One

The Gaze of the Other:
Observation and Testimony

In the Beast's Alley (Poems of conscience)

The Refugees and the Rejected (excerpts)

(dedicated to Malcolm X and Martin Luther King)

Don't wait until the twilight ending,
Until the time of death, time of vital dryness,
When the trees are tossed, blown away, gone
From the innocence of the smile, away to nowhere
For you to claim your grand option for life.

One less moment of love is a huge tragedy,
A waste along the long odyssey of despair
And pain and struggle to re-conquer pride,
Pride of the Sudanese girl or the Somalian mom
Or the boy petrified by alienating wonders
Of a finite world made of matters, manners, finitude!

Deprived of his youth and of a place of warmth,
the refugee is lost, exposed in indifference
On a vast empty land of repressed instinct,
Of delusional happiness;
Condemned to challenging fate,
Reposing new questions along the horizons,
Challenging the vast conspiracy to degenerate the Being,
Our being,
Being there,
Alive,
Real being,
Living in a spiral of inner explosions.

Ready to let destroy the world of fallen heroes,
Ready to erect a vast movement of risen comrades!
Risen Comrades Lumumba, Gaster Raymond, Stephen
Alexis, Risen John Brown, Malcolm X, Antoine Izméry,
Risen the brothers Brissons, Brother Martin Luther
King, Che Guevara, Salvador Allende, Risen Brother
Nasser and Ghandi and all stellar life's lightness
And Brother Chris Hani perished and alive all the same,

Alive, alive,
Alive in the purity of beauty,
The beauty of rebirth.

Along with the refugees crossing the oceans to their death
I've seen death along Massachusetts Avenue, death
On Broadway, along the inner labyrinth of the slums,
Death in Harlem, slum of transcendence, in Roxbury,
Lassaline, South Central or Waco—death of fallen dreams.
I've seen cries, tears, oppression of fashion, perdition.
I've contemplated whole constellations of darkened souls,
Squeezed within the imagination of an inspiring little song;
Oppression has become the ideal, free trade of the mind.
Love has receded to a motion made of trance and folly;
One survives, plays domino, learns the jungle together,
Transcending contingence by a *griot*'s look on the misery.

The refugees and the rejected, sacrificed for a cause,
Have pursued the painful odyssey through a sense of oneself,
Image, and ideal and concept for an already proven lie.
We don't eat our meal in real peace anymore on our Earth,
We don't make love in madness on a vast sunny land
anymore;
We have lost our senses, sleeping in darkness, even with
Back-up computer, bible of a lost memory focused on survival.

After a long poem there's always a long life,
There are you and I, the oppressed,
The rejected who want to clear the mess
and build a new world love order.
Inside the Boeing's cockpit
Or saints of despair squeezed
In the hellish sanctuary of the raft,
Between prison and sharks.
Or on foot and daring the damning calvary of the Rio Grande,
The refugees, grave, brave, headed to the U.S. Hopeful,
From every part of the Earth, via the moon's dark side,

     In the Beast's Alley (Poems of conscience)

Fleeing poverty and despair and cosmic dilution.
They want to shake the world,
Dismiss reality;
They want to die and to live and to let go the pain;
They want tenderness,
Faith in human redemption.

Fleeing horrors and pains from their original lands,
their hearts tormented in new horizons' quest,
dreams lost in the cold universe of the benefactors
they survived by calling their Vodou gods to come
to fight the battle for the Zombie's rebirth,
battle for being in an existence of multiple splendors,
just to play with our people, our children—relaxed!
The refugees came often not just to escape
the withering of a land with no soul and space;
they came to test the infinitude of their dreams,
how to sustain the validity of our shared Cosmos,
how to exhibit hope when confronted by loss,
how to create order when all is disintegrating in pain
—they came ashore from thousands miles of sea
to seek the redemption of our ancestral tribe,
communal unity of land, soul, blood, beauty, equality!

They came and mowed the grass and sowed flowers
of remembrance for the past and an unsure future,
taking shit for the nothingness and the hell that are left;
they came but didn't care whatthefuck you will do
if their dream will cause your neurotic nightmare
to entice tragedy, tears, horrors in our world. No! No!
They came to expand space—the poetic space.

Not quite satisfied of having stolen our world
The jackals deny to our dream our past, our memories:
Would we let them deprive our soul of a future?
Pressed by fate to exist in a meaningless life
We are predestined to an end of total contingence

If we fail to establish our own sense of Essence.
Essence made of disgust for the brutal policeman,
Hero of a badly beaten order of destruction, of grief,
Who kills by habit of sportive and glorious honor.

We must redirect our gaze, our faith in sweetness
Toward the fantasy of infinite splendor, lightness
Of a darkness made of wretchedness, of injustice.
We must go to the streets and reclaim our dreams,
Go and hang around and tell a story and be happy:
Happy in just the feeling of being. Alive. Real.
We will tell their story, our history, our future.

(Boston, 1995)

       In the Beast's Alley (Poems of conscience)

Miamiga

(dedicated to Marty)

Part I. The Sight of a Light

Miamiga will live forever
her shadow from the afar
silhouetting the streets' quiet
along the path to immensity.

She is the crowned hounsi
whose mystique redeems the service
elevating the completion of beauty
through the blind horizon's road.

She is beautiful, Miamiga
elegant meteor from eternity,
vibrating clarity and candor
within the tunnel to decay.

She exists forever, Miamiga
enlightening time and dust and loss
with just her presence from absence
—she will live forever, Miamiga.

(May, 1997)

Part II. *Miamiga has passed away*

Like a fugitive spirit
wandering the hinterland
covered by the falling snow
her red coat lightening her path
she enjoyed the bath in the element.

When on a dark, uneventful night
she told me the previous spring
she was being plagued by a dreadful blight,

she said, "please, please do not cry;
no showing of sadness nor of pain,
I am choosing to live life
with all that is left of my strength,"
I then knew she had found her real fate
and yet I refused to believe that the sun
would go down so soon.

The next time I saw her,
she held and pulled my hand
in a quick and yet tender gesture,
"Come, come," she said,
"I want to show you my dream home;"
a brown, two-story wooden house,
perched between two large and unpretentious trees,
"This is my dream home, you like it, don't you?"
I didn't want to cry
still I was pained by living in denial.

The night that I saw in a Brenda Walcott's play
goddess Oshun surrounded in elevated mood
by her three subliminal, fearful looking sisters
I had the *postmonition* Miamiga was gone;
when I learned it was sure enough what it was
I wished I had had one more time,
one more single instant in her life to tell her,
you know, Miamiga,
I remember your dream
the love and justice you wanted for your people,
I remember your sacrifice,
your pleasure to be there
and your hope it would be a little longer
I remember you were real
as you are for us still real,
you are still alive,
peace to you, sistah!

    (December 11, 1999)

    In the Beast's Alley (Poems of conscience)

Remembrance

(dedicated to Sarah and Aldo)

Remember the old splendid times,
refreshing oasis amidst catastrophes;
remember the smile on your first date,
Sarah's voice murmuring like a dream.

Remember the New York rallies
seeking to save the monster's soul
and the ideals shared in turmoil;
remember the passion for beauty.

Remember the nocturnal walk in silence
together with Sarah in the city streets
or savoring the beach's soothing wind
with a sweet pleasure for just being.

Remember the time before death,
the germinating spring of yesterday;
remember the wonders all around you
she has created for your eternity.

Remember the outburst of fights
and the craving for temporal warmth;
remember what is left from that charm
which has penetrated your whole life.

Remember, my friend, the good times
making love in the mountain's soil,
the common thirst for art's sake madness;
remember her saintly lusty grace.

Remember that life will continue
with Sarah's spirit exhorting and leading
the invincible battle for world peace—
Remember that we need you, my friend.

(Cambridge, May 18, 1996)

Thank You Asteroid

*(Once in a while, the poet is inspired by a
historical calamity or a cosmic catastrophe to
ask a question—his or her own question. This
poem expresses my organic feelings about the
alarms steered by the possibility that a destructive
Asteroid may be heading toward the Earth.)*

I am in ecstasy
happy we will all be gone
to the abysmal nothingness
we merit as a grace.

I am savoring in delight
my vengeance over the Suckers
who refuse to my soul a refuge
I enjoy my glory!

Come on! my dear Asteroid
my companion on the other side
of what is not and now shall be;
come on! my cosmic terrorist,
replace the finitude by the infinity!

I am in ecstasy
awaiting for the dinosaurs' return
from the impact of 1997-XF11
the land before past time
will return in our time.

I sure will miss the human smile
the prairies and the green mountains
the new-born's first smile
the whisky in the carnival
love in the dark of the night.

   In the Beast's Alley (Poems of conscience)

Come my dear Asteroid friend
exorcize the evil spirit of the Earth
reestablish the primal element
in its authentic and magical rebirth
come redeem the loss of the soul.

The medias will no more spy on us
despite the huge interspatial radar
they will launch to pulse the tremor
sense the infinite secret of the Asteroid
renewing the vital spiral of life.

In the eve of our global destruction
I call on my brethrens in chaos
to create a new land of renewed splendor
vitalize the virginity of the contingence
elevate the surreal beauty of the lost land.

Pécheresse of Freedom (Desire)

My mind wandering aimlessly
on the podium, and the poetry, the clamor
nagging the prudence of my hot desire,
amour, I thought of you—smiling beauty.
My anxiety changed into *rêverie,*
desert into forest—Spring renewal,
Eden remade for the fulfillment
sacred fulfillment of the naked fresh,
irradiant *soleil* in the winter's grip.
Return! Welcome return to the spirit, my dear,
erotic, flamboyant *pécheresse* of freedom!

(Cambridge, 1/22/1997)

Enemies' Symphony

(dedicated to the "gang" at the Thirsty Scholar)

The unbelievable feast
the unreal happenstance
putative enemies
dancing in make-shift dance-hall
a river of smile
replacing a river of blood
replacing different spades of skins
same blood
but look like two different species
the enemy is everywhere
in a river of blood
on a road to nowhere.

Wait until you cross the Rubicon
even for a less dramatic cause than Caesar's;
wait until you join the enemy
in his quest for the redeemed question
and sing along together the last song
and ask for the news from the front;
the limbs destroyed and dreams deferred
beauty in fugitive, furtive encounters
building continuance in absence.

I have enjoyed the dance
the community in the soul
the donated space for transcendence
people in communion
I have enjoyed the dance
and the soul-searching.

An asymmetric boxing duel
transubstantiation in evildoing
the alterity of the instant
changing the carnival

from good to bad
or bad to good
and bad good as US democratic alternation.

Baseball as an excuse
boxing as metaphor
but real harm is being done
still we are singing along
adversities connect
instead of being a hindrance
to the devilish tone and goal;
we are dancing along
because there is only one life
mine and yours all the same.

Putative enemies
yet the heartbeat is the same
the blood all the same red
human fate in action.

Ours was the ether world
offspring of the old time
we were children in rebellion
we longed for something in between
between total madness
and total rejection;
we longed for the human touch
the state of no non-sense.

One said the blacks were all bad
and the whites not too far off
another said the jury is still out
one called the girl demonic temptation
another made her a beautiful saint
we had different points of view
but we knew war is to maim and kill
even when beautiful lyrics enhance its appeal.

    In the Beast's Alley (Poems of conscience)

Putative enemies
and companions in madness
still dreamers for a time of illusions
and ideals made everyday miracles;
we shall build our own temple,
glory for beauty on earth.

(First published in the journals *Tanbou-Tambour* and
Auscultations, 2006)

Welcome to the new-born

Welcome children, welcome!
We welcome with our hearts
and our arms wide open
your young souls and your smiles
under a freezing sun
in an abandoned land
land of drought and no wind
land of no food
land of no home.

Welcome children, welcome!
come with your joy
come with your spirit
to lessen the lot of the lost *loas*
come with your drum
come with fresh water
come to the *Gede Nibo* dance
come to the land of no smile
come embellish the hell!

(Boston, May 1995)

Thanksgiving 1994

People assembling over clamor and laughter,
Over the dreadful map of macabre USA.
Cadavers mounted around Thanksgiving tables
In the agitation of happiness, joyful reunions,
While the decor was surreal, grandly sustained,
Immersed in the infinite of contingence.

The news and the menu intertwined
Rebounded from time to time at a glimpse
Through the kitchen table and the rolling TV:
200,000 dead from the war fronts
Balkans, Palestinians from Hebron
Israelis on a bus
Holocausted Jews returning from the dead
Thousands are wiped out by the tempest Gordon
On top of the ones from the military might.

Millions of children,
Innocence perverted by horror
Go through life as an ephemeral morning dream;
They die the next day
Along the streets
Forgotten.

The news rebounded with vitality around the table,
Filtered through the waste of the mortal turkey:
Rwandans perished in sportive machete mayhem
Dead in nothingness
Away from the bankers,
Far away from the simple taste of a quiet life.
Away.

The news bombed the air waves but failed to detonate
A huge cry of rebellion to break the conforming paradise
Of a dead universe of terror—poisonous space.
The news rebounded, channeled by its grandiloquence
To establish symphonic cohesion of the faith
Between immolated homeless and artists of bad faith!

The news more and more has become exorcism
To mask women who are killed by love's tenderness,
People who suffer in the very joy of life's survival
roulette.
Children are mistreated
Sacrificed
Decapitated
Put down
In their innocence to invent a more human madness.
The children are gone
To economize energy
To save time.
The news rebounded, invading our privacy and right:
The teen-age mother will be sterilized
Stripped of sins.
"Three strikes and you're out,"
Purified of imperfection.
Out to hell
To the frigid ash of your animality!
And the teens would silently join the corner street gang
Out of despair
And need for renewal.

The news rebounded with sensational charm:
Mothers kill their offspring by boredom;
Fathers have deserted the family's land.
Fugitive.
They want to save their sanity
To regain hope in life.
Schoolchildren bomb teachers, principals and pupils,
They shoot at the moon to ignite poetic creativity,
They burn archives and libraries to save memories.
The news comes with shock, surprise and fear:
The sharks will no longer be there to kill,
I won't miss their piquant killer's flair,
I'll be spared one more deep sea massacre!
I'll renew the spirit of life's palpitation!

    (1994)

        In the Beast's Alley (Poems of conscience)

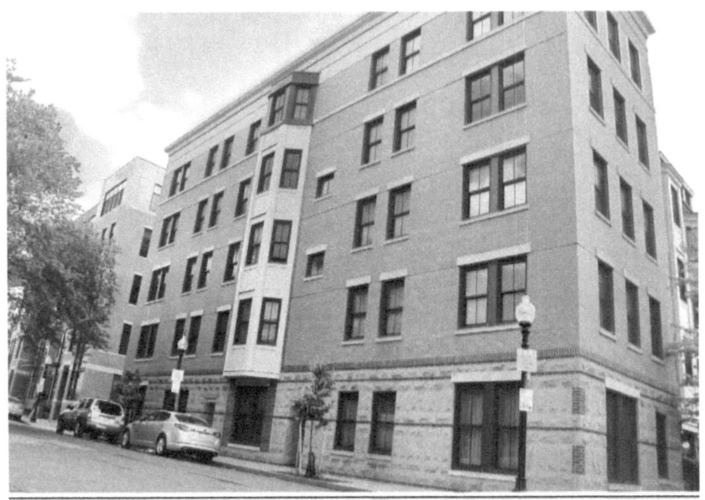

A luxury apartment building near the Franklin Street Park
—*photo by Patrick Sylvain, 2013.*

Despair

(dedicated to the Klu Klux Klan and Jean-Marie Le Pen)

"The White man is angry" said the news,
Angry for becoming God at his own expense;
He's bored in grim alienation,
His imagination has reached zero degree.
He's angry, my man,
For losing to lowlifes.
Don't advise him to drink himself to death;
No recourse except a poem of despairing faith
Will reshape a soul so disturbed by loss.

The news rebounded
Matter-of-fact like a divine dictate:
No more love-making under the tropical sun;
No more flirtation with strangers in dark alleys;
You shall make love in daylight
On the highway of shame.

The news resounded with provocative clarity:
The military farm will only produce MRE
Meals Ready To Eat with diabolical promptitude
Peace of the mind.
No more family farm,
No more individual seeding
Or private gardening:
Nutrients will be dispensed through computerized network.
The next menu will be futuristic
The food succulent,
Soft, tender, oily and juicy
But no real human tasting will be allowed,
Appetite and preference are out
Full stomachs in
If your brain is not blown out!

   In the Beast's Alley (Poems of conscience)

Upon hearing those terrible news,
I retreated for a while to the soul.
I retreated to my tomb,
To my original despair
I thought of my son to be born and said:
Too bad, the USA!

"The White man is angry" they said
From which quarreling clan of this loss
And vast tribe of the human jungle is that man?
Is he the factoryman in Belfast,
The brickmaker in Boston?
Is he from the clan that gazed six million Jews,
Or that one who killed Palestinian children
And Iraqi elders?
Is he made of Napoleonic glory to live life in subliminal trance?
Is he Rimbaud or Himmler who tried to break the whole premise?
Is he Beethoven who played by the flair of genius?
Is he John Brown who conspired with Harriet Tubman
To destroy the master's old house
And build in its stead a freedom?
Is he Guevara or George Mason,
Infernal deity of people's anger
Or Angel of death?

Is he fear, wisdom or dream or Newt Gingrich?
Who declared war on poor people's right to a decent life?
Is he Sartre or Marcuse, de Beauvoir, Eleanor Roosevelt,
Norman Mailer or Tom Paine?
Or holy species of crazy *entendement*
Such as Castro, Gorki, Genet, Hoffman, Lorca or Jesus
Who have perverted life to save the ideal of beatific eternity?
Is he my buddy Tom Phillip
Who curses to hell all emotional non-sense
Only to sacrifice his fate to the pain of transcendental
hopelessness?
Is he Jacques Brel or John Lennon
Madonna, Trotsky or Lenin?
Or a Jack the Ripper trapped in the dead-end madness?

"The White man is angry" said the news,
Angry for his lost space
Under the weight of his claim to dominance.
His soul has reached the sky of emptiness
Diluted in undarkened whiteness,
He is light in a desert,
Vast land of hell
Whose twilight constitutes its only joyful gift!
He's angry, the White man,
No more tropical beaches,
No more ski country;
He won't be seen anymore smiling on the moon
En route to Jupiter,
Happily mystified by ecstasy.

Which one of the white man's clan is designated
By this claim of purified perdition
And non-being?
Is he that one who kills in the shadow,
On a night of despair
Or my cousin Lev who travels the Atlantic
On a piece of wood
For one last chance to fortune?
Or for a simple last smile?
Is he the ones who invaded a deserted land
And declared victory on CNN
With Peter Arnett showing the horrors?
I won't miss this man
Who's creating hell to save humanity
Nor the faithful one
Who's selling me bills as my holy bible!

"The White man is worried" said the news,
Matter-of-fact like an algebraic law,
Soft and logical;
His world is invaded by threatening barbarians. Alas!
His center devastated by a mosaic of broken consciences

                    In the Beast's Alley (Poems of conscience)

Ready to place the blame for unfulfilled chimeras.
He's angry and of course rightly so
For his conqueror's right:
He's beaten by the teen-age mothers
And the boys in the 'hood!
Humiliated on his way to godliness,
An irrelevance on the pile.

Pile of people's yells of disturbance
To mark a day of birth,
A day of strike of cry
Of laughter
Or of death,
Or of light
Infinitude in a world of repressed souls
And military happiness in the desert!

"The White man is unhappy" said the news
Disoriented in the spiral of boredom
While his Black counterpart is locked in the shortness of time;
Time redistributed through the prism of consequential
profit
Where respite, refreshment, rejoicing or love in dark alleys
Are punished by virtue of family values
Celestial bullshits!

"The White man will be gone" said the news,
Gone to the insignificance of ephemeral eclipse.
Contingence on a populated map
Of evaporated geniuses
And dreams reached deflated,
Castle of paper,
Great Panopticon occupied by nightmare.

He's gone, my superman, my hero,
Toward the end-limit of human history,
Gone with the wind and the swing;
He's no longer the Man, the only human;

He's as white or black or bad as my shit
He's my man
My blood
My evil twin.
I will miss my White man
Angle of a shadowed rainbow.

(December 1994)

                    In the Beast's Alley (Poems of conscience)

O.J. and Me: The Take of the Poet

First, a warning: The following poem was composed before the not-guilty verdict concluding the criminal trial of O.J. Simpson. Naturally that verdict ruined the poem, since its credibility and authenticity rested on the firm assumption that O.J. was guilty as charged, conformingly to the circumstances presented and alleged during the trial, and taken at face value. Therefore the O.J. here discussed is a fictional O.J., reinvented by my subjective hypothesis of what the truth is, independently of the legal judgment or of the *real* truth of the matter.

Second, while the subsequent verdict by the civil court ruling Simpson's "responsibility" in the death of Nicole Brown and Ronald Goldman has somewhat reinstated the credibility of my guilt assumption in the poem, it also left me angry by the realization that *justice*—as search for the truth and correction of wrongdoings—was being perverted by people's emotions and perceptions, and by the Machiavellianism of the arcane justice system. The death of Brown and Goldman was not really properly adjudicated per se at the end, neither, possibly, were the perpetrator or perpetrators irrefutably proven and punished [although, in the light of O.J.'s subsequent release of a book, *If I did It,* that apparently implies he did it, only a fool can seriously believe in his innocence].

In any case, as with the Von Bulow or the Rodney King cases—and regardless of its application in instances that pleased our ideological bias—a justice system which needs two trials (with two opposite outcomes and two sets of standards) to establish justice, must be a system of injustice. Whatever our empathy for the stricken families of the dead and our admiration for a father's strong-mindedness in single-handedly seeking justice for the death of his son, amidst tremendous odds; and however captivating were the theatrics of the drama or demeaning was the process, the Simpson's trials have demonstrated, if anything, that the US justice system remains a Janus, with two faces: One for the poor and one for the rich; one for Black and one for White; one for men and one for women; one for the politically connected and one for the excluded. A justice system unduly influenced by the multiple relations of power in the socio-economic sphere of human interaction, creating a general climate of mystification and untrustworthiness, thus disproving US society's ideals of itself as a nurturing unit in the pursuit of life's splendors.

Despite our fundamental differences in wealth and material acquisition, O.J. and I have a lot in common. He is Black and male, so am I. He is an athlete, I am a poet: We both deal with elements, space, time, contingency, hazard, dreams, and speed. Speed? Rather *mistrust* of the fast lane-life, for my part.

When I first heard the news of the murders, I cried for this one more romance turned hellish and nightmarish. I cried for Nicole, this beautiful woman—who was once an innocent and angelic girl—when she faced her assailant, with his look of perdition, destruction, full of mortuary passion. Her sudden life's ending let me with a bitter feeling of a life stopped by un-necessary, un-needed and arbitrary situation. Had she woken up on another day, in different circumstances, his gaze could have been one of joy, beauty, inspiring trust, pleasure, a sense of showering in the sun, caressed by the wind, wind and

     In the Beast's Alley (Poems of conscience)

hands of her man, handsome man, charnel creature who would tell her: "I love you." I also cried for that young and innocent man, Ronald Goldman, who was apparently put, by the contingency of a mere chance encounter (or unbeknownst to us all, by other mysterious causality), between the crossfire of passion and destruction.

I also cried, of course, for O.J., that man who suffers in silence, in the deepness of his soul and heart; a man who has lost everything that is really dear to him, including his own connection to himself. Despite my assumption of his guilt of the monstrous crime, I empathize with his terrible loss, for this man is the most miserable one among all the tragedy's protagonists. Faced with his own conscience, probably exclusive receptacle of the ultimate truth, he becomes the undesirable hero of an unwanted drama that transcends his own apprehension of the unfolding events. He becomes an object, passive figurant in a worldwide absurd theater. A fallen hero.

Of course, a fallen hero doesn't a fallen destiny make. As the philosopher Jean-Paul Sartre said, one can always *make something different*—by mere will power, by a claim of freedom or a sense of drama,—of what is prescribed by the existential and social determinism of the existing social order. O.J. was sociologically destined, both by the structural construct of this order, and within the historical confine of the time, to be at best a hustler, possibly a resigned poor man, but certainly not a hero. His short-cutting foray into becoming a celebrated sport hero didn't erase the fact that his success only illustrates the rules of the game: The chances are not every single Black man in the United States would become a sport hero, even though they'd want to. In any case, sport is a safe category that doesn't need much soul searching. It's a spectator's pleasure activity for which the personal odyssey of the athlete is totally irrelevant, much less his political or historical context.

As was the case for most famous black athletes, notably Muhammad Ali and Nascimento Pelé among them, the Establishment's acclaim for the black athletic hero is always lived as a phenomenal, exceptional, even accidental occurrence, which together satisfies its phantasms of glory and its need of a contented self-conscience. Interestingly enough O.J. Simpson and Malcolm X come from, basically, the same historical, ethnic and social background, but while one was celebrated by the so-called mainstream Establishment, the other was perceived as its worst nemesis. While one has inoculated his soul with the fast lane splendor of the American dream, the other launched himself into the unknowns of political rebellion to force justice on the land and freedom for his people. Both are, however, survivors of the same dysfunctional, socio-economic reality from two different angles.

That one was killed as a martyr and the other vilified as a villain, says a good deal of the US spectacle culture. Make no mistake, however: their common blackness is just a small part, a referential epithet in the overall signification of the drama. The fact is that most downtrodden men and women of this society—be they black or white or yellow—share the fundamental alienation of these two men's destinies by the constant tick-tack of validation between success and failure, representativity and exclusion, acknowledgement and oblivion, celebrity

     In the Beast's Alley (Poems of conscience)

and invisibility, poverty and *wealthiness,* necessity and contingency, plenitude and *incomplétude,* being and nothingness.

Neither the old-time chivalry of the noble classic era, nor the chic of the Post-modernist, nihilistic dogma of today, has a remedy for the soul. Killing for *my* love is no different from killing for *my* property or killing for *my* glory and *my* image: the well-being of the soul is despondent of the nutrients with which it has been fed. Emptiness creates artificiality which in turn creates alienation and heartlessness.

Ironically, independently of his ultimate guilt or innocence, we make O.J. hold the key to our understanding of what occurred that fateful night: but he can also fool us by claiming either innocence or guilt. The sadness of the situation is that whatever the truth behind the dual verdict will prove to be, O.J. will always have to deal with his losses: the loss of a woman he loved, the loss of his children's trust, the loss of his status of hero. Hero or villain O.J. will never again live in peace. [This prediction made in 1995 would prove premonitory considering the many legal troubles he would later find himself in.]

Naturally, in this matrix of virtuality and reality interceded in a symbiotic madness of wealth, power, sexuality, racism and plasticity, love ceases being a simple joy of being in the company (or the memory) of the beloved Other, be they a sister, a cousin, a friend, a lover, or a spouse; it ceases being the joy of experiencing a moment of transcendental elation with any beautiful human being who brings to your personal existence a little human warmth.

In the end, stripped of its cosmic element, unrepresented in the high drama, love's "got nothing to do with it," as the Tina Turner song goes. It becomes an expression of a narcissistic game, a manipulated pawn in a relation of power—as if love the tender, the sweet honey, love the subliminal splendor, love the erotic trance, happiness translated in a feeling of actual well-being, had created a kind of alternated malicious sublimity, a transubstantiated eroticism made of human negations. That this deviated love would kill on a certain day when it is faced with its reflection of existential boredom, its lacking of purpose, its emptiness, its *incomplétude* of being—that is not a surprise. It will kill because it finds itself far away from the soul, penetrated by terrestrial impulses, taken by a huge force of total destruction. Alienated.

Alienated by a cosmic and social epistemology within the confines of political expediency, for which fundamental issues like life and death, suffering, happiness and human destiny are de-validated, relegated to fantasy category, dismissed as doctrinal orthodoxy coming from obscure preachers lacking the right credentials. While, of course, humans are being marketed as computer data, stupid consumers for whom no manipulation technique is absurd enough to demerit their monies—and their souls.

Today we are already being designated for mass human cloning. Perhaps we will need no mother's mound, her uterus, her nourishing breast, nor the father's sperm or parental wisdom, to make us grow and prosper. Can we break away from such a nightmare and build a new human perspective based on the assumption that we can recreate our lives conformingly to our liberational aspirations? That is the question.

   In the Beast's Alley (Poems of conscience)

Very fortunately, the human spirit always reaches a certain breaking point where it cannot take it anymore, and acts to change the mess—be it in a decade, a century or a millennium. Human cloning, human marketing and human devaluation may be the most trendy achievement that is offered to us today, but we also know that the concept of human redemption—cherished by the religions—is the same as the notion of liberation cherished by the revolutionary movements: a stage of *humanization of life,* which together encompasses and reformulates all adventures, misfortunes and aspirations of the human soul toward the realization of the dream of being.

We shall not return to the Stone Age because we invented High Technology; we must however use High-Technology to help realize the dreams of the Stone Age. After all, why would we want to clone a multiplicity of the same when the sample is in such a state of dismay and decay? It's sad that the Simpson story was such a compelling story of our time. This world of ours would be a much better world if we had devoted the same amount of attention and concern to the plight of the homeless as we had devoted to the problematic of O.J.'s guilt and innocence. The troubles of the factory worker who has no future in a system of structural exploitation; the confusion of the teen-age mother denounced as a sinner in a society of pseudo-parental virtue; the nightmare of the homosexual deprived of a nurturing space; the ghetto girl and boy excluded from the American Dream; the immigrant lost in a virtual and multilateral reality that devaluates his or her sense of being; the proud woman trapped in the male-dominated world of so-called penis envy and pussy reification, would be better off if the O.J. story were just a story. By default of a more nurturing and humanized cosmos tending to real human happiness, we made of the O.J. story our story, while, in fact, it is just the illustration of our nothingness. There must be another way.

In the Beast's Alley (Poems of conscience)

Elegies to the Simpson Madness

He killed her one hundred times before
when he told her he loved her as a bird
lost in the wonderment and madness of being.
Adventurer in hell trapped by his own ego,
he descended into the pavement, his soul
had forgotten the path to the infinite space,
to the vast cosmos—celestial transcendence.

He killed because his heart was petrified
by the nostalgia coming from the time passed;
time of love under the pine trees, in open sky,
sensual and sweet moment of ultimate pleasure
when the unity of being and the grace of her flesh
were in enamoring trance with the sun.
—He killed when he was no longer just a dream.

He killed because killing has then become
the purest expression of the male's power trip,
ero-sacrificial ritual for the fucked-up lovers
bent on destroying the pleasure principle
just to place their unhappiness in a museum.
He killed when beauty was an ideal no more,
when his heart changed suddenly to stone.

He killed when he became a prisoner
restricted in the confines of a miniature cell,
narrow road on a too fast a lane to nowhere,
to the infinite finitude of a morbidity
escaping the artificiality of the naked matter.
His endurance had conquered the magic
only to let it sleep under a zombie spell.

He killed when his love told him in disgust
that all will from now on be a disaster,
dreams changed to nightmare; hailed freedom
for a regained dignity of an oppressed soul,

would end at the tunnel of the Impossible.
O! Valorous courage to attain transcendence
within the nothingness of a dead-end corner!

While the elixir of the Simpson's drama
was instilled in our veins of spectator guinea-pigs,
soon as the spotlight was on, fixated on the scripts
of myopia and self-hate hailed as entertainment,
you and I were reduced to primal contingence,
ideal consumers for marketing scheme
—happy recipients of soap-opera epics.

While we were dazed off by the Simpson's pills
zealous legislators were deciding in silence
of our fate and virtues for the next millennium;
innocent men were found guilty as charged
because of their profiles of terrorist bandits;
groups of tenants ended up on the streets
due to downsizing of Wall Street's junk bonds.

Mortuaries of broken bones, dry tears,
children killed in absence, their dreams depleted,
betrayed within the bureaucratic grandiosity.
Teen-aged mothers were made the enemies
to scapegoat scandalous bilking of the civic trust
by those who take our world as their own domain.
This was a time when suffering was made a crime.

In this diabolical mess smiles changed to swears
while love was reduced to mundane etiquette,
the ideal family was thrown trough the window
for mass consumption and anthropophagy
of a public conditioned to applauding bad-taste
—Magnificence of mediatic happiness,
defiance, defeat and death of a sad romance.

This had begun a long time ego, since the time
when the proud profiteers were made the saviors

                    In the Beast's Alley (Poems of conscience)

of the exotic land—aiming for spatial conquest
and redemptive prayer for life's degradation
in usurped lands and souls, death in the desert,
amid laments of despair of whole communities
whose souls were eaten by hunger and pain.

It began when we killed the dream and installed
in its stead a computer center to quantify progress
and disqualify whatever emotional in-put
or humanly feeling which distracts production.
After they had killed the ideal and the dream,
the law of the jungle became the mainstream,
global madness, false ecstasy in a hellish Nirvana.

Hatred for the self and the Other's self, eternal
purgatory in Bad-life—and killing will follow,
for we are being told that is the only way, the way
of a soul so distraught that it needs to destroy.
The cops might have been happy, adrenalin risen,
to have hero-figure O.J. feed their prejudices
and keep peace on the land without a fanfare.

O.J. has reincarnated what he was made to be
from the start in a hatred-dominated world,
world of losers who kill wives and girlfriends,
deviants who make love under a freezing sea
beyond the frontiers of Apartheidized lives
and who kiss and yell and dream and cry,
living in constant displacement and defiance.

World of teen-age mothers giving birth
in vast cemeteries paved with grey boredom;
metamorphosis of a boy in an asshole killer
or a pimp who uses charm to collect his dues
and terror if love failed to impose blindness;
surreal manipulator with majestic prestige,
athletic hero edge from Hollywood canon
—phantasms of a universe with no dream.

Celebrate all the protagonists' histories,
but leave in peace the dead and the living
who share the emptiness of common fate.
The O.J.'s tale is not our history—it is
the lost memory of our depravation;
the mountain's cloud hiding the beauty.
Who will sing the song of the awakened dead?
Who will throw the first stone at O.J.?

(Boston, 1995–1997)

In the Beast's Alley (Poems of conscience)

Supplication to the Killers of Children

In the midst of total nothingness, absurdity and despair, I want to continue to believe in something, to still have hope in tomorrow, hope that our children will have the option to make of this world of ours a better place. It is with this desire to be part of the solution to madness that I wrote the following poem.

The poem is dedicated to the children you have hurt, killed or intended to kill, but it is most of all addressed to you, to the beautiful children you once were, but who at one point decided to hate people instead of hating the human-made adverse conditions and structures that alienate your lives.

The path you are leading us down is a dangerous one, for if we continue to demean not only other peoples' lives but also our own and those of our children, we will surely condemn ourselves to extinction as a species. Perhaps this is what you want all along, but think twice, does it really make sense to you? You may be crazy, but you are not a fool.

To all those of you who want to kill just for the hatred of the Other, I ask: How would you feel if your prophecies and goals were really fulfilled? Would you really like a world of "only you," only one color, shade, one physical feature, one representation of God, one single song, one literature, one single expression of love? Do you really want a world of only one truth, one book, one horizon? A world where you have the moon and not the sun, the plains and not the mountains, the lands and not the oceans, the rocks and not the plants, hate and not love, death and not life? Do you really wish for a world of sweet and honey without the spices, the aroma of hotness, the libidinal high of salt? Perhaps; but you surely will be bored to death.

While I may empathize with your anger and unhappiness, and the darkness that fosters your despair, there is absolutely no reason to hate or harm people you have just bumped onto, much less little children who are relying upon you for guidance and support. If you, personally, really think harming them will further your cause, your lost, demented soul needs help right now. Open your heart to the person dearest to you or the moral figure you happen to respect. Please, do it now; do not wait! I want to reach you in your inner soul, your humanity, for you are still a human being entangled in circumstances you may not have brought upon yourself but on the demarcation of which you still have some control. Remember what the French philosopher Jean-Paul Sartre once said: One can always do something about what society or circumstances have done to one.

If talking to someone doesn't work, and you still feel the impulse to harm, do this one more thing: Go to the nearest ocean beach, bring enough food and drink for only one night; Lie half-clothed on the sands and watch the day and night go by; let yourself enjoy the wonders of the sun, the calm of the moon, the changing shade of the weather and the vast freshness of the water waves; take the time to reflect on your dreams as a growing child, the pain you have endured; think of all the small good deeds you have done and the grateful smiles you saw in their recipients' faces; think of the people you have hurt and of how deep in yourself you wish things were different;

In the Beast's Alley (Poems of conscience)

revive the people you have loved and the unforgettable joy they have brought in your life; think most of all of how a simple decision of yours would save many lives, avoid unnecessary pain, and thereby, perhaps, contribute to the evolving fulfillment of a promising life. Continue and repeat this process of self-inquiry until you feel ready to go back to a human village—any human village—and help toward the betterment of living. Otherwise, stay on the ocean beach until you are ready or until Mother Nature recycles your body in the soil of her infinite re-nourishment of life. Perhaps that earthly transition was your true mission in life.

Please, do not harm the children

*(this poem was first dedicated to the children and
the other victims who were shot and wounded by
a racist gunman at the Jewish Community Center
in Los Angeles on August 10, 1999—I also dedicate
it to the children who were wounded and killed by
a gunman in a Amish schoolhouse on October 2,
2006, in southeastern Pennsylvania, and to the 22
killed at the Sandy Hook Elementary School in
Newtown, Connecticut, on December 14, 2012)*

Little gentle hands
as if playing ring-around
joined in unison together
entrusting to the adults' guidance
their lives and fears and dreams.

They were born just yesterday
a time when joy was for them possible
they came with their vulnerability
armed if only with their hope
to receive our blissful offering.

Burn as long as you wish
the mountain will not go away
destroy all that is still living
our memory will resurface one day
and life will still be our lot.

Please, do not harm the children
you can for your tormented soul
sow new seeds to grow a new garden
tell your grand-children a new story
share the pride that makes you cry.

   In the Beast's Alley (Poems of conscience)

If you feel you must kill—kill instead
the nightmares that engulfs our world
exterminate the pain that blinds your horizon
the darkness that festers your despair
the miseries brought by human avarice.

Please, do not harm the children
those angelic lilacs of infinite wonders
breath the same air you inhale and pollute
reclaiming your wisdom and boredom
inheriting the deepness of your roots.

Please, do not harm the children
remember the cute child you once were
the marvels you wanted to conquer
the smiles you fostered on many sorrow faces
remember tomorrow is a new beginning.

(August 1999)

Memories and Tributes: Ideals Under Boots

*(dedicated to my friends, the former counselors
at B.A.S., a shelter for teenagers)*

Soldiers of human kindness
they were there to only let live,
to help the dream follow its course
or to simply smile in wildness.

The boyz in the 'hoods, tragic characters,
along with angelic girls of the suburbs,
congregated around the hoods' shelter;
even the beautiful birds of the hostile cosmos
would come here to give birth, the eggs securely
sheltered on the house's back porch.

Idealists of a new way of being but also
genuinely confronting their own ego's impulses,
inhabitants of all walks of life's deserted lands,
they joined in unison to sing our world's sonnets:
they cried, they laughed, they dreamed, they were.

They were there, when Reagan was killing the dream;
there when Bush was annihilating the land,
a land occupied by big bucks, by intolerance
and by the zombifying glamour of Hollywood chic;
land of desubstantiated souls, of happy yuppies,
where crap is valued as social charity;
they were there, my friends, to rebuild hope.

Vivid examples of our societies' wrongs,
the children shared with the graceful workers
a communal destiny against the system's grip,
they shared the victimization along with the hope
on a huge empty map peopled by bureaucrats.

Preston X would fly through the whole universe
to find a girl he would love and pursue;

In the Beast's Alley (Poems of conscience)

he is Stendhal's antihero in love with love,
never mind he's more beautiful when *chilling*;
he chills to let go, to let the mind blow,
simply to see which way things would go.
Henri IV, his roommate, was a monk at fifteen
who mastered a system of musical control
that rejected the pretense of the holy notation;
they joined Keith VI the Italian, shocked and proud,
to create a rap symphony of eternal wisdom,
whose violence barely hid the cry for tenderness.

My first day at work was with Julian the *Griot*,
taciturn, calm, permeated by a profound knowledge
of the ways and prehistory of the entire place,
he taught me how one survived tragedy on Earth.
Julian never spoke a word without deep thinking,
he seemed to be torn between indifference and fate.
For now, on my first day, he said "Hello" gently.

Queen Daniela, rebellious like the ancestral goddess,
would shake things in a feast of total destruction
to make the simple point that she was a human being!
Sole inheritor of her fate, she chose the dramatic exit,
before returning to a new assault made of a single smile.

Through the shelter's windows, through its doors,
the world reverberates with its sense of despair,
but we refuse to cry because all is never lost,
there's always a new way to reclaim our lives.
The celestial flame of people's resistance
continues its pursuit of regeneration.

Nobody should be hurt for being an innocent kid,
nobody should be hurt for being there to let live;
the projection of power by the system's horrors
should not target people who are there to help:
I protest the constant trampling of human ideals!

Shelters can be a depository of Hell;
my friends the counselors made ours a home
where human empathy is shared with great courage.
They sensed that our world needs a shake-up of souls
or a quiet place where the torrent will rest. Torrent!

Lost in pain, deserted by all in apathetic hypocrisy,
there suddenly brightens, looms as a purgatory oasis,
a respite altogether bad, good and naïve,
to the children of hope looking for new spaces;
our humane presence was our only weapon.

In the end and despite the infinite misery
that surrounded their lives, despite the horror,
these kids were the most beautiful of beings
ever engendered on a huge empty land;
they projected and reflected a calmness in turmoil,
a vast richness of supreme transcendence in shit
that make them a challenge even to the Creator.
Some of them ceased to *boom* in the hostile 'hoods
and chose to *boom* instead with candid good faith;
they joined the shelter and the staff in defiance,
defiance to save what still could be saved.

Without a home, without a bath, without a friend;
without rights, justice, freedom or dignity,
humans are rejected, degraded in the elements.
Without a companion's smile, without a human face,
we would lose the reason for us to be alive to fight.
In the end, small mercies like ours must join the torrent
to yell a loud cry for justice, for love, made of beauty
in the dream of being every day celebrated.

    (1993)

        In the Beast's Alley (Poems of conscience)

Promethean Parables*

In Cosmos' alternated movement
the sun will follow the rainy days
itself radiated by refreshing
new offspring
even after the peaceful sleep of the night.

In morning's temperate occurrence
propel both a furor and a calm,
calm of the eternal *nanm*
the actual presence of what there is
the ephemeral glare of the instant,
the episodic storms of rebirth, the poise
of nature's passionate embrace.
Engendered by contingence's dead end,
sedated under its spell and smell,
only human glorious desires
will transcend the Animal Farm
disfigured by bestial instincts.

Inside the death chamber
or on the hospital bed
the song of freedom retains
its lasting appeal toward being
while beauty remains
the source of authenticity.

Even when the body is ravaged by pain
the spirit still relives its sensual candor
elated by convulsive spasms of joy.
The stressful and mischievous days
may give rise to new revelations,
mortality itself becoming just a crossroad
where the ever tragic destiny of things
reaches its point of illumination;
your nurse becomes the Goddess of light
both the impossible nature of being

and the natural and cosmic wonderment,
perhaps just a fugitive moment of happiness.

As the storm must follow its trajectory
and accomplish its dutiful damages
the sensual gaiety of the spring
reveals its most sacred affirmation;
the withered, dead-end mechanic element
has now rejoined the inconsequential trash;
the ruin is everywhere
still the Cosmos has regained its balance
and retained its profound wisdom
amidst the forceful vitality of life
there was renewal
spreading fire
and the return of the fresh morning.

Blessed with her Promethean freedom
the abortive mother, new Mary Madeleine
keeps her alternative between Superwoman
and Nature's call to save the species;
she dreams of peopling the new Universe
with rebel minds of all passionate faith.

The Sun's light has filtered Death Row,
redeemed the prisoner's short life;
his finitude has changed to the Eternal,
the infinite fluidity
the elemental conscience to judge
together God, the Capital and the Fatherland,
anything that was being sallied
everything glory has not yet perverted.

Just like the innocent and tender infant
would brighten her smile for the criminal
the most bestial may not have the last words.

The end doesn't exist

                    In the Beast's Alley (Poems of conscience)

false invention of tired spirits
searching a last hurrah to nowhere,
while a thunder road would do.

(November 2000)

* First published in the anthology *Poets Against the Killing Fields*, 2007.

In the Beast's Alley (Poems of conscience)

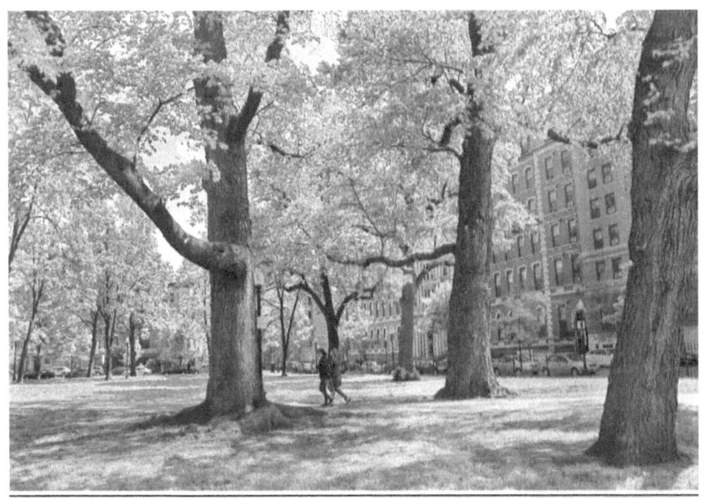

Boston's Franklin Street Park —*photo by Patrick Sylvain, 2013.*

A Genuine Disgrace

(dedicated to Juan)

He was a true rebel
my fifteen year old lion,
robust just like a storm
and calm like the death
he wanted to join in disgust
for a life of pain—non-sense
coming all around his cage.

His heart was bleeding
with chagrin for living
in an elliptic world
confined fugitive
within contingence
and absence;
his youth has repelled death
for life was so much part of him.

Red blood on a dark cloth
even his depression was a passion
to challenge the end-game—a vow
to reaping what is left from nothing.
He knew his power was a mirage
and his mother the reigning regent
who left him the burden to lead Rome
without a compass for guidance.

He knew life was an absurdity
to which his madness gave meaning;
he refused to be the sacrificial lamb
for values that were not his wanting.
When he said he did not want to live
I told him that he had no other choice
—he despised my logic
although he liked my gut.

    In the Beast's Alley (Poems of conscience)

He said, man, no more school for me
I said, man, I will surely call the cops,
when he said, go for it make my day
I said, well, let's find another way,
he replied that there is no other way
I said, you don't look for one yet—
and his look conveyed his incredulity.

When he said, nobody cares for me
I said, you are just one of them;
when he made of suicide a relief
I said, your life is still a miracle;
he said, please let me go to my fate,
I said, your dreams are also your fate
but your mom will forever be pained,
he retorted, my life is mine to die for.

One teacher once told him
that I am a disgrace to mankind
for not being her ideal bureaucrat
he retorted in kind:
"My man is genuine."
He was taught to hate even his own soul
I told him he could blow off the bullshit.
He wanted to go to the darkness of death,
 giving up to his damned spirit—I said:
Wait, brother, for the little instant of beauty.

(Cambridge, 1997

Ayibobo* for Brother Mumia Abu-Jamal

It's a great day to hope
well into the row's nightmare
in the darkness of pain
and tears through the body's pores
betrayed by the sun and light
confined in the solitary hole of silence
away from into and under
society's spell and living in hell
deprived of the aroma of food
and spirit and spices and sweetness
and salty joyfulness of sexual goodness
all gone to the abyss of the row's madness!

Oh! Today is a great day to hope
that this forest-born man of nowhere
last blood of the deep Congolese line
that this voice of nowhere
voice of the *desperados* voiceless
voice from the madness of being
voice of Mumia our comrade
will penetrate our abused conscience!

Mumia's metamorphosis from hell kid
to coldly cop killer and hero in death row
was already being plotted for fateful demise
since the beginning of the trap to harm hope
harm its element of fire
until *l'enfant terrible* jumped back to yell!
Yell his innocence by virtue of cosmic truth!

Whomever may this scourged soul be
that took Officer Faulkner's life on that day
in full boastful *viva* while blood paved the ways
is now lost somewhere in despair
part of the pathology of collective killing!
Whether you kill or let this Mumia live

    In the Beast's Alley (Poems of conscience)

his specter will continue to haunt
haunt our memory our space our peace:
"I still sojourn in hell"
said he dreadfully the day of the stay.

It's a great day to hope, hope indeed
that the delirium nausea of horror
and the street-level holocaust of our dream
in that morbid day on a Philadelphia street
where souls that fight
children that dream
birds that fly
and MOVE people reclaiming humanity **
were calcined in great indifference
gone in flames
and blown away in words of beauty
words of the beatified soul of death
words of what is said and is done
words of media enlightened hatred
will cease their strangulation of destiny!

It's a great day to hope
that Sacco and Vanzetti will rejoice
and reclaim death's greatness
in their graves and their *nanm* ***
and reshape the ideals of being.

It's a great day to hope and demand
that we stop the slaughter of life, stop
the dismantlement of energy, light, horizon!
A good day to banish sorrow
or life in death row or any society's row:
Hopeful is the day of Abu-Jamal's freedom!

(August 1995)

* *Ayibobo* is an expression in the Haitian vodou rituals
  that means literally: "Hail to the spirits."

** MOVE, a radical Black politico-spiritual movement
whose headquarters were bombed and burnt to the
ground by the Philadelphia police department in 1985;
11 people were killed, including children, 53 houses
destroyed and 265 people made homeless by the blasts.

*** *Nanm* is a Haitian word meaning together soul,
spirit, consciousness, intelligence.

　　　　In the Beast's Alley (Poems of conscience)

My Christmas

My Christmas
is the slain Christ lying
on the cross defying
the jackals of the time.

My Christmas
is the Jew in a Warsaw ghetto
waving a last kiss to her newborn
en route to the pogrom's madness.

My Christmas
is the caged bird escaping away
toward the unknown of infinity
simply to taste a day of freedom.

My Christmas
is the Palestinian from Gaza
dreaming of regaining his lost land,
growing his vegetables in the sun.

My Christmas
is the smile on the homeless' face
conquering the surrounding horror,
genial impostor of impossibility!

My Christmas
is the youth from the ghost cities,
tender spirits circling the desert
seeking encounter with the wonders.
They sustain the balance of Earth
and renew the season of life's dream;
they spiral into the deep firmament
jumping and yelling and asking for space,
light in the labyrinth of nowhere.

My Christmas
is the refugee from the wretched shore

reinventing a map for enchantment
and saving the essence of the species.

My Christmas
is the other face of the deal,
the requiem for those lost fights
for a more humane fate.

My Christmas
is the rebirth of the dead souls,
the rebellion of the dormant spring
against the rampage of the fallen leaves.

My Christmas causes no harm
and no broken hearts and spirits;
my Christmas is the joy of the day
the beauty of the passing instant;
My Christmas
is your smile
your tenderness
our follies.

(December 1997)

The Deluge*

(dedicated to Abbie Hoffman)

I see coming a time of painful cries,
A time of huge calamities after today's torpor.
I see coming from the background of our era
The rehabilitation of the dreadful evils
Who don't give a fuck about our bourgeois conscience.
I see coming against all expectations
Also a time of timeless love,
A time of priceless ideals
When Beauty and humanity will become one pursuit.

Hey! tell me: Why all these vain clamors?
Why have you always told me that I am
A failure or a bum because I love and dream?
Why have you killed the man who only asked to live?
Why are you refusing me the right of being different
Of this Establishment who corrupts all ethics
And perverts life itself to please the dandy?

All along this passing century
We've learned to enjoy life without tenderness,
We've learned to mourn our people's anguishes
Without questioning the responsible cause,
If it is God or man or our stupidities.
Hey! tell me: Why all this carnival of tears?
Why this woman, this man and this child
Have no home to stay and no friend to visit?

Why have we shot this man?
Why is this exploited worker denied a future?
Why do we have to cry in silence and alone?
Why did this sick woman have to die alone
By lack of an insurance policy?
Why do millions of starving people have to die everyday
When a supersonic Concorde can be there anytime?

This is a catastrophe!
Our shameful resignation!

But even in the middle of absolute nothingness
Life for me has always retained a taste of springtime joy.
Hey! Let's burn down the Babylon's temples!
Let's burn hypocrisy and get rid of the tricks!
Let's go, together, as a disrespectful torrent
Spreading the terror of our damnation!
Let's march against Wall Street and the White House!
Let's invade the satanic churches who use the gospel
For the only purpose of sweetening our angers
To prevent our revolt!
Let's live tomorrow together against today's hatred
The everlasting spring of our Renaissance
We will build together in love and happiness
A beautiful town rich of flowers and sun.
Let's realize together the liberated labor,
Which will re-establish our total dignity.
Come on! Come on! my people of sorrow
Lets' destroy the jerry-built house of our oppressors;
Let's destroy the decayed cattle of these death advocates
And build instead a city of Rock n' Roll. Animated!

Then, when the tears are over,
After our conscience has re-learned to fight
And to take human beings as its first principle
Against the temptation of a huge bank account,
We will find that we are nothing but a mistake,
A highway accident far from a State trooper.
Then, when the show is over, naked, decadent, unmasked
And even Hell itself has become a routine,
We will find that we had missed the call of Destiny.
But if we know today ourselves as a miracle of being
We can recreate a whole new set of human relations
Where Earth, Water, Woman and Oxygen
Will join in symphony to sing life's mystery,

   In the Beast's Alley (Poems of conscience)

To start again to dream without computer,
To be able again to love without Hollywood,
To become real. A simple little bird.

* First published in *Street Magazine,* 1990.

My Life

I was born ten thousand years ago
with my soul immersed in evanescence;
I cried to express and yelled to convey
a rational tempo in a craze to living.

I am the hurricane
the blowing wind of destruction
passing through the immense forest;
I am the flood
the blood from the injured membrane,
the tempest from the dormant ocean.

I was born to live
and die in my intensity
part energetic impulses,
part dreams
part of you
part of what is not yet and shall be.

My life is a multicolored entity
blue wall, red exit, gray nightmare
erected to confine my wonders
in the jails of routine production—
removing the spirit of its beam, banning
celestial beauty from the arts' follies.
I reinvented in protest a freedom
based on life's rebirth
and its irradiance.

I am both a dream and a curse
spiraling around and beyond destiny;
I am a vagabond—a human eclipse.
I walk along the edged street's curbs
to avoid being a distracted customer
away from my muse and my dreams
—from afar the missing element.

    In the Beast's Alley (Poems of conscience)

I live to be there
and breathe the air of life
I go with the wind and against the flow
of the meaningless spatial enclosure;
I was meant not to be
I was born embedded in a thorn bush
between who I should be
and who I really am;
I am a ghost
a fugitive moment
an orgasmic cascade.

I dread imagining my son
being part of this universe of non-sense
I sing him secret songs of freedom—
he is my glory and my pain in infinity.
I refuse to enjoy the blasphemy
of life and simulation in a cozy embrace;
I am the product of an accidental release
spilled in the dark of the night.
I am a fluid sensation
an electron of nerves
from the defunct Stone Age;
I am the memory of time;
a Poet with nowhere to go—
I am an impossibility
a huge question mark.

I have made of my Pantheon
a longing for the taste of beauty
but I hate a society which acclaims
the beauty of the dead at the museum
and the glory of the beast at the Bourse;
I hate all post-modernist zombies
the guardians of temporal madness;
I am a meteor from nowhere,
I am an illusion
a rebellion
a celebration.

    (Nov. 1996)

The Eternal Elemental Poetry of Things

The poetry remains the same
even when the muse is no longer
your guardian angel in hard times
and the elements are disintegrated
and sore like a carnival of madness.

The poetry survives
the early morning fights
and the bad news from the front;
it survives the body depleted
in emotional plight
and the last cry.

The poetry survives
the eternal purgatory of things
the bills that are not paid on time
the sojourn in back alley dormitories
words drowned in seas of non-sense.

The poetry survives
and revives the sun's vibes.
while permeates the Monday blues;
it survives the evanescence
of the fugitive moment, the flesh
that has changed to dust
and the full moon full of passion crime.

The poetry survives
the killing field as it transcends
the prisoner's last meal on death row.
The poetry survives the last breath
after everything else had gone.

The poetry will survive
the materiality of life's end-game
and the eternity of its illusions;
it will survive both its shadow,

                              In the Beast's Alley (Poems of conscience)

its metaphoric finality
and the blood shed in real time.

The poetry will survive
the atom of irrelevance
the solitary voice of the Desert's Griot
yet still a powerful presence.

The poetry will survive the wrinkle
and even the end when it ever comes;
it will survive the nuclear age
and the kingdom of the Market lore;
the poetry will survive everything
even the end.

(November 2000)

The Tide and Tayitae's Smile*

As the clouds spread
engulfing the horizon's view
the constellation lost in total eclipse
rainstorm flooding the nurturing space
dead spirits all around the *vèvè*
decay in Michelangelo frescoes
twilight to the midnight hour
the sun pierces through invisible holes
penetrates deep into the inner soil
to bring new nutrients to the trees' roots
all becomes possible
carnival in the town square
dreams revived by beauty's spell
the nightingale is singing again
on the open and verdant plain
food to the hungry
peace to the land
liberated spirits
renewing life's cycle
the spring has come
with a beautiful smile.

(July 1998)

* First published in the magazine *Auscultations*, 2008.

   In the Beast's Alley (Poems of conscience)

Pseudo-Haikus For Immigrants Haters

*(dedicated to millions in the United States
who mobilized in March–April 2006 to
demand equal rights for US immigrants and
immigration-originated families that have been
the mainstay of US society since the beginning)*

Lou Dobbs, Major-Jon in his CNN perk
immolates his own people's spirit
in a time of lament and fits.

The Mayflower's descent in wretchedness
found in the new land a respite
the same Columbus acquired.

Germany's "guest workers" and the like
few years after the Final Solution
convey lessons in bashing absolution.

The *Mexicans* have come back home,
would you think since this land was taken
a day the Rio Grande was in blood and mayhem.

You say "Go Home!" I say "Go Home Too!"
We all come from a nether space of despair;
I say "Let's All Together Come Home!"

Ranting may well protect your stuffs
other peoples exist in our world
Cosmos turns around and conscience still molds.

Racism degrades the eternal meaning
the cross-germination of recreated beauties
you may want to return to time passed.

Time when the liberation dream of being
even in the absence of genuine love rituals
regained the right to question and to hope.

(March–April 2006)

If You Make Hussein Prez

(dedicated to Barack Hussein Obama)

If you make Hussein prez
You'd betray our 4th of July
You'd ally with genuine patriots
To seize the helm of the Capitol.

If you make Hussein prez
Fred Douglass would smile in his grave
His words having made the rounds
Even in the heartless Capital's glowing lore.

If you make Hussein prez
I would hold a party for Malcolm
And have John Brown make it a ball
though Wall Street takes off with the dough.

If you make Hussein prez
You may make the KKK cringe
Although some adherents would applaud
The time's urgency for boldness.

If you make Hussein prez
We will sing God Bless the USA
And call for ML King to be there
To celebrate the potency of his dream.

If you make Hussein prez
You would humanize evilness
And make political-ethical humanism
The law of your tormented land.

If you make Hussein prez
You may not adjure centuries of misdeeds
By those who have milked our Cosmos
But you'd defeat pettiness for pettiness' sake.

   In the Beast's Alley (Poems of conscience)

If you make Hussein prez
You'd change your destiny in the process
If only by showing despite all Fox's folktales
That you are not twentieth-century Great Moron.

If you make Hussein prez
You probably voted for your own interests
Instead of the corporate farce
Serving as hide-out for greed.

If you make Hussein prez
You defend the honor of your land
Saving your country from horrors
After many decades of privatized State.

If you make Hussein prez
You probably know his name is Barry
He is a Christian not a Muslim nor a Buddhist
Not a Jewish and not a Vodou Hounsi.

If you make Hussein prez
You probably want to stop the BS
And the coziness and the *thieveness*
Stop more bleeding from the wound.

If you make Hussein prez
You'd regain a rejuvenated life
Reaffirm multiple splendors of the races
Redirect destiny and *changer la vie.*

If you make Hussein prez
You probably won't change anything
Only the color of the Beast
And the bitterness of the poison.

(October 2008)

In the Beast's Alley (Poems of conscience)

Part Two

Power and Tribulations

In the Beast's Alley (Poems of conscience)

Ode of tears for Gaza

After missiles were launched
after roads cut in two
that lead to nowhere
after unrelenting alarms
of ambulance sirens
taking the injured to remote hospitals
and silence returned dread like a curse
after the razing of whole neighborhoods
walls turning to ashes
bones tossed in communal fosses
and even dogs are deprived of water.

After all hospital beds were taken
and the mortuaries were full
sacristan devoid of farewell songs
seeds that cannot grow
no rice bowl on the dinner table
and meal served when good luck smiled.

After schools were closed
and no one was told
after one family lost brothers
and sisters and mothers and fathers
and cousins and next door friends
after blood became to the soil
to the streets and to the inner soul
just a flowing and fluid element.

After there's no more places to run
after homes become for teenaged IDF*
fair game targets in competitive sport
after children were crying for hunger
ribs exposed like in the butcher's stand.

After you crossed the land
threw bombs around in fury

like pigeon feeders do for crumbs
after our livelihood was destroyed
and guns shot at emergency first-aid
and the town market closed down
carved in rivers of tears and pain
no more social security office
no more hang-out at nightfall.

After doing all that you wanted
to keep them from ever existing
after you have used all weapons
to silence all voices that say no
you remain an empty shell
still haunted by your bad spirit
still crushed under the weight of fear
still threatened by world wide oblivion
still entangled in anxiety.

After all you have done
to in your memory avenge
the deportation and exile
the gas chamber and despair
your people had endured
we can together join in Earth's memory
and share millenaries of tears and dreams
there's no monopoly in Odyssey land
none of us is the Universe's lone member.

Even after decades of ordeal
Gaza still stays alive to fight
she is not responsible for your curse
nor is she the hell you put upon yourself.

Gaza is not Hamas
but Hamas is of Gaza made
voting for the government you want
isn't it what democracy preaches?
Voting for the government you want

                    In the Beast's Alley (Poems of conscience)

doesn't mean only if big powers approve.
Where there is no justice there is no peace
we all are forgotten children
following Earth's compass with blinders
all massacres are the same
be they done in Gaza
in Ramallah in Qana or in Haifa
whether they take place in Fallujah
in the World Trade Center
or in the Site Solèy.

Gaza is not Hamas
but we are all Gazaans
untamed conscience that struggles
for the right to a better future
the right to decide what we want.

Israel has caused death needlessly
this is the truth of the picnic incursion
Gaza is not New York nor Philadelphia
nor Washington DC or Boston
still the blood shed interpellates us all.

Killing in hours masses of souls
is a war crime in Auschwitz
as well as in Guernica
as well as in Srebrenica or in Gaza
to change is to stop defending
with a tortured yet straight face
Israel's atrocities regardless
change is to ask for that to change.

Gaza is our inner sin
conscience and memory of history
memory of horrors that shouldn't be
memory of the need for justice
conscience for liberated Gaza.

Pain should unite not divide
history and memory of horrors
far from being alienating hindrance
to manufacture reign of fear
could unleash flowing waves
to our common humanity elevate
we shall cry for all our dead
let us join on the road to new hope.

(January 2009)

* IDF = Israel Defense Forces.

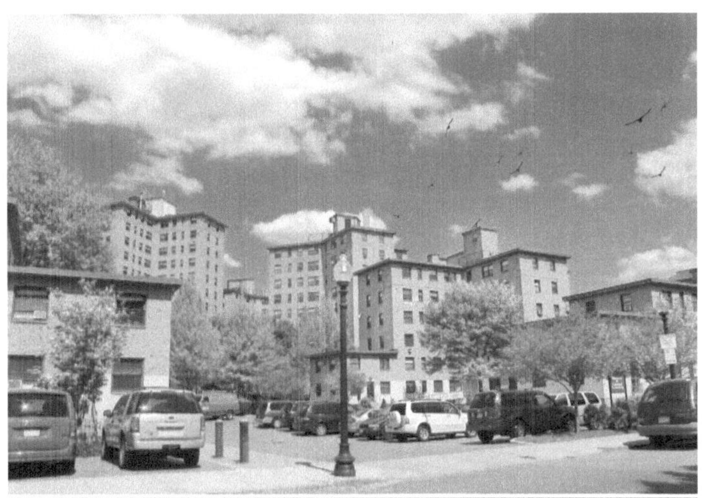

The Cathedral Housing Project —*photo by Patrick Sylvain, 2013.*

Dying for Kosovo

I would die for the crying child
who woke up parentless in the night
entangled in the cold of the mountain's grip;
I shall not die for NATO's ego trip.

I would die for the Albanians thrown out
from the refuge of their land,
fathers executed while the dinner is served;
I shall not die for the small club's glory.

I would die for the desperate mothers
who sold their innocence to save the family,
the young men sacrificed for wardom rituals;
I shall not die for the empire's creed.

I would die for beloved Kosovo
for the memory of the Illyrian tribe,
for the birthplace of Serbian nationhood;
I shall not die for the New World Order.

I would die to avenge the Serbs killed
in the train, on the bus, on the bridge,
for those who never woke up from their sleep;
I shall not die for the Greater Serbia.

I would die for a womb aborted of its cells,
its corpus estranged in six warring parts,
I would die for beauty to come back to the land;
I shall not die to make the war machine stronger.

I would die for a borderless world,
infinite horizon to new revelations,
I would die to have rock' n roll in war zones;
I shall not die for the Dow Jones's rise.

I would die for the renewal of our dreams,
for the ties of sisterhood sustaining the despair,
I would die for justice for all the rejected

   In the Beast's Alley (Poems of conscience)

of a world consumed by power dominance;
I would die to stop the killings
in High School as well as in our soul;
I would die to plant trees
all around the Big Dig of Boston;
I would die to move to our backyards
the graveyards, the penitentiaries
and the downsizing factories
just to give us a feel of the war.

I shall not die for the bullies' exhilaration,
for the big voice that calls all of the shots,
I shall not die for your bad faith;
I would die for no more bombs.

I shall not die for the Pentagon's sweets
selling us the angels of the sky,
killing like God-sent crusading saints
whole villages of unrepentant Serbs.
Nor shall I die for a humanless enclave.

I would die
for a kiss
for a smile in death row
for food on the table
for school for all children
for the end of despair
I would die for Kosovo
and all of its peoples;
I shall not die for NATO's goals.

   (May 1999)

Jenin

*(dedicated to the memory of the hundreds of
victims of the Israeli army's April 2002 massacre of
Palestinian refugees and national liberation resistants
in the Palestinian town of Jenin, in the West Bank)*

I. Cadavers from a long time passed

They invaded in long lines
geometrical incursions
for diabolical aims;
they invaded with uproars
made of mortuary laments
Jenin, Ramallah, Nablus, Gaza had to go
along with their people
the siege didn't last
as long as the valiant people's quest
for Allah's pleasing
and for freedom quest!

They invaded in long lines
of handsome *commandeurs*
orderly positioned
as Roman Centurions
helicopters and tanks
that demolish with skills
the best manual on hand
on how to best kill and maim
without leaving traces
except perhaps the brownish
darkened flattened houses
cadavers from a long time passed.

They invaded in long lines
of dream-destroyers
memory-erasers

   In the Beast's Alley (Poems of conscience)

the people had long veins
and deep roots;
they came in long lines
amidst the children's cries
with goals to break the spines
of all that is still breathing life.

They invaded with intent to demise
millenaries of bond and spilled blood
for the spirit of the lost land;
they came in long lines
the people had built their own shrine
and a long line
of peace makers
and suicided-bombers
a long line
of dreamers.

They invaded
and put pain under siege
no water and no meds
no light and no sight
no life
piles of pain
under curfews that last
as long as evil deeds could.

They invaded to break bones
blow up houses and kill all living beings
seeming too invested in ideals and dreams
they came with a plan
for diabolical aim
they came with a plan
and the people had their own.

II. Real Blood For A Peace With Justice

The pavement looked like a red carpet
of real blood from broken bones
seen as rocks in a surreal enclave;
houses burned and bulldozed
killing point blank
with no regrets
convoys of hurried tanks
and piles of dead rebels
and not so rebel dead
a.k.a. terrorists for the sake of the cause
the almost extinct
but always renewed clan
in Fatima, Mohammed and David's land.

The pavement was also made of tears
on the other side of the sacrificial lamb
a proud and beautiful people
had made the butcher its savior
and the tanks its God's prayer
the spoiler had entered the sphere
a mortal punishment.

A human bomb is always a tragedy
and denied rights are still rights
we shall heed the despair of a soul
so entangled in pain
and in giving pain
all victims have the right to be
and being.

One shall not subjugate
and hope for happiness to flourish;
the powerful state is obligated
to the sake of human wellbeing
the spoiler had entered the sphere
so had the critical conscience.

   In the Beast's Alley (Poems of conscience)

The Palestinian people will be free;
it's the fate they had chosen
since the beginning of the fight for life;
the people will be free
that was always their call.

(April 12, 2002)

The Saviors From the Cold

(dedicated to the people of Iraq and to world peace)

They will come tomorrow
or today or anytime now
they are all powerful
and that is not even the question.
They will come tomorrow
because they have already massed
in martial posture along the beaches
and the borders
in the desert's sands
and on the mountains' top
on a night of cold
and that's not even the question.

They will come tomorrow
because they have the means to come
and destroy millennia of wonderment
and keep hope entwined with despair
and love from entering life's sphere
and the adrenaline in stupor and awe.

They will come tomorrow
because their well-suited angel of madness
had opened the door with his own topping.
Will they see where the bombs land
and the torsos pierced on a sunny morning?
Will they hear the voices
from the old and new coasts
resonating the craving for world peace?
Will they hear the children cry
amid the smoke on torched balconies?
Will they hear justice cry?

They will come tomorrow
because they must grease the machine

     In the Beast's Alley (Poems of conscience)

which programs them to come
and affirm the nobility right of the Empire.
They will come tomorrow
regardless of the number of dead
the aim is not to let it be.

They will come tomorrow
and ours will be defiant cries
calling for the re-conquest of liberated space;
we must stop them before the vultures
from the sky could claw whole villages
we must stop them before the end.

I've seen the oppression of the tyranny
I've seen the desert Bedouin's crimes
I've also heard the war roars
the tumbling of the tanks
the missiles and the technologies
the cleanly degrading from afar
of peoples' parts and universal right;
I've heard the bulldozing of the bamboo stems
which stood in dissent on the road to conquest.
I've heard the painful moans
from the loss of the dearest ones
from the hurt of the last lost war
many distances away from the hometown,
I still mourn the passing of Gerry The Jovial
who joined the "beautiful adventure" life offers
in Air Force just to flee the neighborhood's curse
and eat on time in friendly macho posse
and pay on time his lofty college cost
only to return in a bag with a flag
after being made enemy for a cause
that was not even his from the start.

I've seen young crops lost
wasted like my deceased siblings

in subtler societal war madness
denuded of war lyrics in dejected horizon
they will have died before the time
nature had offered for their use
after the long lines at emergency wards
amidst losses and pains amidst the penury
stomachs full of the emptiness of being
complication from surgical targeting
Belgrade in flames
Kabul in ruins
Baghdad depleted under uranium shells
the cries of bored children
countries succumbed to the Bully's charm
burnt oil fields
increased malnutrition
and infant mortality
and dropout dumbs
inflational gas price
kids killing kids
laid-off minimum wages workers
welfare to work to mouth
glory of the angry white men
and nights without super
mornings without breakfast
nights without sleep
souls without space
blood on the sands
tears everywhere
is that the war your want?
your war
O beautiful war!

The killing field has many faces
the fearful Republican Guards decapitated
by earth-shaking missiles as well as
First private Suarez or noble Sergeant Gutie

    In the Beast's Alley (Poems of conscience)

along Second Grader Shad and they all died
in huge sandstorm of mortal furry
incited by the fire power of the enemy;
some died before the new fatherland
had made them its full sons or before
new sons had met their new fathers' faces.

They will come tomorrow
at the dawn of hope's birth
they will come with engines of death
high-tech at the uses of delusional claims
and oil envy with planetary grain.
They will come
and that much is now sure
but we shall block their trajectory's burst
and spare the abolishment of human pride.

They will come tomorrow
and we will be millions strong
in New York to regain the memory of our death
in Paris to make sense of chaos
in Conakry to redeem the ancestral soul
in London to keep Russell alive
in Cairo to pity the sold-out princes
in Santiago to avenge Allende
in Mexico to purge the affront to Castro
in Port-au-Prince to save what is still left.

They will come tomorrow
and we will be there to sing hope
and ask for new constellations;
they will come tomorrow
and we will be there to claim peace
expand daily beauty without the non-sense
they will come to sow and shed blood
and we will be there to open new roads
they will come tomorrow

and we will be there
to demand justice
and the joy of being.

(Boston, March/April 2003)

In the Beast's Alley (Poems of conscience)

Similitude*

(a poem for peace)

As its shadow
in its inner sanctum
casts its last pall
the sun retreats to the beyond.

Still it's the same time,
you know, on the other side
even in different shades
the same time in Baghdad
the same time on Park Avenue
the same time in the slums
same madness and same hope.

It's the same blood,
you know, like the other soul,
the same artery in Shia
the same on the Sunni side
the same on the Christian side
the same in Haifa and in Qana
the same in Gaza and in Ramallah
the same in Philly and in the Bronx
the same in Port-au-Prince and in Kabul
the same even with the Infidels.

It's the same pain,
you know, just like other mothers
the same sleepless nights
the same hope of waking up
to a less awful truth.

It's the same dream,
you know, like any other hopeful spirit
the same trepidation in opening the letter
the same hope that beauty never fades.

It's the same time
the same blood
the same pain
the same creed
the same family
the same madness
the same dream
the same illusion.

* First published in *Auscultations,* 2007.

Free Soul

The huge Eagle of the greenish dollar,
Airborne 82nd and friendly marines
Landed in the heart of broken Port-au-Prince;
And people sang and sang—Viva democracy!

I was hurting inside deep under my bones
For not being able to happily naïvely celebrate
The defeat of my country on this lovely day
I refused the alchemy of guns and bread!

Duped and mystified I'm glad my people
Hold again the hope of a liberated land.
Veye yo! Veye yo! they call from consciousness
For a vigilant soul to save four hundred years
Of dreams and struggle. *Veye yo! Veye yo!*
Free we will be again. Free as the angry torrent!

(1994)

What Would Old Breda Say?*

*(dedicated to Toussaint Louverture
in commemoration of the 200-year
anniversary of his martyrdom)*

He had sworn seven times
since life past in his ancestral Ginen
to the dark dungeon in Jura's Fort de Joux
through Napoleon's in-law's court
for liberty's roots to stay alive
even on the road to nowhere.

Old Breda would want the island's brave
penetrate memory since the original agony
and find solutions to the warring curse
within a family string-pulled at will.
Old Breda would have wished
for the plantation's offspring to aim high
even when Suckingall wants discord
among all of those who sing hope.

Old Breda didn't cry
even when cheated and deceived as he was
by Hédouville's play of Rigaud's aims;
Old Breda would have been pained
to trade dawn for nightfall
and for the demise of respect and fairness
of people for people
and country for country and people
even when Uncle Sam's wrath obliges.

Old Breda would call
for Jean Dominique's death to be avenged
for Noriega to be released with an apology
for food to eat on Easter Sunday
for justice for Sandino's heading to his death
through colonist deceit be made an epiphany

     In the Beast's Alley (Poems of conscience)

of people's rights and beauty and human dignity.
Old Breda would demand
reparation for Charlemagne Péralte's death
and for the island's fate centuries past Leclerc
that had brought imperial might for right
be made a testimony to glory.

Old Breda would not want
Iraq to be made a pretext or a saint
nor for the museum library bombarded
under raining missiles in Arabia
be made an imperial glory to cherish.

In Jura's dungeon
Old Breda swore for his star to brighten
and for constellations in dark alleys
to become the lightning rod
and for liberty's praises be loud
he swore for all of that which had passed
would not come back to haunt justice's quest
Old Breda would call for peace.

What would Old Breda say
if two hundred years have not brought
a flowering oasis of multiple wonders
in the heart of the plantation's ills?
What would he say if the sun turns dark
if the nightingale has not sung at sunrise?

What would Old Breda say
if the people lose hope
faced with Bonaparte's double
faced with the stubbornness of fresh feeling
for old ills and fresh blood for burnt past?
What would Old Breda say
if Antoine Nan Gome is made pope
on a Baghdad square
live on CNN in open air?

What would he say if our cry for help
fall on closed hearts?
What would Old Breda say
if "boat-people" thrown out
return to the island
and build something grand?
What would he say
if Port-au-Prince were blocked
by liquidators with smile?
What would he say
if the lost memory were to come back
and Haiti were again our pride?

What would Old Breda say
if Maswife doesn't climb the pole on January 1st?
if basilica can't destroy evil curses?
What would Old Breda say
if the roots are withered and depleted of nutrients?
How happy would Old Breda be
if we break open a new dawn?

    (2003)

* First published in Revolution, Révolution, Revolisyon:
An Artistic Commemoration of the Haitian Revolution,
edited by Ella Turenne, 2004.

The Water That Nourishes
And That drowns

(The majestic Eagle and the return
of the angelic Rooster)

The slander, high-aiming and majestic Eagle
Criss-crosses and flies over hills and mountains
Smiling in a conquering gait, while the people
Happily celebrates the Rooster's return;
The whole thing wrapped in troubling surreality.

Magnificent scenery as was the divine protection
Of twenty thousands marines with delighted gaze;
Magnificent scenery still conscious will remain
Those who transcend the moment and see the beyond,
Defeating the conditioning of a violated conscience.

The president is returned, celebrated by his people
This was its great demand and a great victory
On this unsettling, anxiety-fraught regime of shame.
The president is returned, and the people sings and sings;
Let's hope again the dream doesn't change to nightmare.

Alas! the people's throat-cutters hailed from everywhere,
From fortified barracks, as from data-resplendent,
Air-conditioned offices; they are from deforested
mountains,
the universities, the ocean's other side infected by our
dead:
They reincarnated today as well greeny greenbacks!

The Eagle of great sentiments, of conquering glories,
Unique super-thief of the fair, beautiful angel of hope
Bursts irresistibly in the heart of the valley of pains;
It has regained its soul in Port-au-Prince's belly. Princely.
The wealth of the place sold by auction. Cheaply.

The president is returned, and millions of broken backs,
Badly ripped open chests, families and women violated
March on the Champs-de-Mars, breathing refreshing air;
This victory is theirs despite the powerful Eagle.
Fruit of their smarting in turning the 82nd Airborne.

I am afraid they may dupe them again, oh great people!
Bare-footed from thorny path sacrificing the symbol
Like they once burned down the city in defiance to horror
To save hope and drink a bowl of milk, well rested;
Tranquil rest of the sleeping bear. Domesticated.

This was stressing my heart deep under my bones
For not being able to celebrate my people's joyful defeat
In this Pyrrhic victory that smelled the poison,
I fear they would betray again its dream of liberty!
Let's sweep and sweep away all the soil's toxicants!

The ceremonies are just exorcisms and blindness
Masking the macabre behind smiling faces.
After the performance, after the melodious clarion,
After the mediatic hype announcing highly dreams
Still will remain a great need for the air and the sun!

Just like the oppression and the terror inflicted
By a horrendous regime have bestialized humans
The State of law that accepts willingly being enchained
By a cajoling Empire that is trampling its ideals
Enjoys the nourishing water forgetting the drowning one.

While duped and mistreated the people is never blasé;
It holds still even when mystified by the enchanting oracle
Of the guardian angel-like Eagle and the *virtual reality:*
If it contents itself of the crumbs from this unjust sharing
It would wake up in a vast *tyouboum!* *

Victorious is the people that sows its freedom from the sap
Of defiance of its own resistance to oppressive forces.
Against fear, against terror, against servitude's emptiness

   In the Beast's Alley (Poems of conscience)

It holds its principle, its intrinsic rebelliousness, red blood,
To reinvent ecstasy, to regain the liberated space.

On the run, defeated, humiliated, and booed by the people
A clique of the horror squads takes the luxury exile road,
escaped away in the failed dictators' in-service jet,
And the people sings and sings, and thus life continues.

They kill us with intoxicating savior preaches,
With the sword inspired by the cemetery peace;
We are dying sacralizing our own strangle-hold
Of shadowy images embellishing the living nightmare!
If they are really gone, why have we lost our vision?

Let's watch the spaces conquered from burnt lands;
The great joyful day is a great funeral wake
Of futures trapped in the instant's euphoria;
Let's watch the enslaved's fair chained up to the soul
In Big Brother's dogma passed for miracle-maker.

The horror is replaced by charming deception,
The great stoup of rebel is now great advocate
Of order nicely officiating to reconciliation
Between the good and the absurd in a huge mirror play:
We are being sold cheap charity for our own mercy.

A look from afar, over the dense frog of the view
Is our only light in the quest for meaning in the abyss;
Free are the woman, the man and the rebellious child
Who look for answer in the audacity of risk:
Those who look for their souls the path is often full of thorns.

Yes, we will be free tomorrow on a plain purified
Of marines, and of the thugs and throat-cutter classes
That obscure oppression under the guise of ideal
In a theater of the absurd and mystifying scenes:
Free we will be one day—free as the torrent's wave.

* *Tyouboum*: Trouble, serious problem, calamity

(This poem, written in 2010, is the English translation of
the Haitian poem "Dlo n'ap bwè k'ap nwaye n," written
in 1994 in protest against the marine-escorted return of
Haiti's exiled president Jean-Bertrand Aristide)

     In the Beast's Alley (Poems of conscience)

Rest For The Warriors*

(dedicated to Gadi and to peace in the Middle East)

1. The conquerors

After the last combat
you will need to rest
O dear soldier of my glory days!
After you had conquered
thanks to your valorous might
the land we have both coveted
and the gold that sustains its pride
you have left me empty
devoid of hope
yet still expecting something else.

The nourishment of my youthful dreams
has withered, faded away,
in its stead a calvary of pain,
of broken bones,
blown away flesh,
tears in faces that could no longer smile,
soulmates separated by the ocean's width,
families petrified by losses,
has invaded my soul.

Dear soldier of my glory days,
you have left me in the cold;
our villages have become fortified barracks,
shopping malls carved alongside the minefield
and oasis of well guarded quiet cemeteries.
Still we remain companions of the same time
and space and peoples' aspirations toward
new camaraderies in non-lethal follies;
we remain companions in everyday discoveries.
Come and retire your gun, my dear soldier
we now need you for much deeper ideals,
come to redeem the fight.

2. The conquered

After the last fight
the fight to reconquer our lost lands
we were left with our dreams while our everyday life
was filled with worries of not let pass at checkpoints;
fear of being left behind in employment lines,
panic for not knowing how the next meal will come,
life in deserted land
time spent in inhospitable jails
tears that never seem to dry.
After the last Intifada
and the last blowing up of busses
there comes the time to heal;
after the last land reconquered
we will still need the people to be there
all the people.

After the last fight
you will lose your coveted land
but you will retain your dreams
and a human space in a tormented soul.
After the last fight
shall come the lasting peace.

3. Peace of the Brave

The skin that is burnt or beaten or pierced
could be of any shade of pigmentation;
the instrument of evil is color blind.
Yesterday was the Jew's sojourn in hell,
today is the Arab's turn;
but his funeral changed from tears to spear.

Tomorrow will be a day of curse
if the warriors for peace let the way to Sharon;
the Jew will again be made the enemy

   In the Beast's Alley (Poems of conscience)

while the Arab will remain the Savage,
the hate-monger will have a filled day
at the expense of human decency.
We may never erase from our memory
the Arab boy killed in his father's arms,
nor the two Israeli men lynched as a ritual sport,
nor Rachel buried alive under the bulldozer's wheels.

But one should have the courage to say no,
no to the killing of people by a powerful
army right under CNN's glare;
no to the might made right and the humiliation
made as a policy just to degrade the soul;
no to the destruction
and the burning and desecration
of the schools, the synagogues and the mosques,
no to the occupation of stolen lands
and yes to the existence of Israel.
If evil will have the upper hand
if the Israelis will remain the conquerors
if no one will stand up for justice
if the Jew is made the scapegoat,
then we must say there's no hope.

But if I shall cry for our losses
or for what we will never have,
I ought to believe peace is still possible
France and England after all
once fought one hundred years of war.
Palestine will become the land of
all its peoples and their faiths
and their dreams,
a land of peace and justice
a land of love.

* First published in the anthology *Poets Against the Killing Fields*, 2007.

In the Beast's Alley (Poems of conscience)

Part Three

New poems and new horizons

In the Beast's Alley (Poems of conscience)

The Automaton at Sandy Hook

*(In memory of the 20 pupils and 6 teachers
killed at the Sandy Hook Elementary School in
Newtown, Connecticut, on December 14, 2012)*

He has our natural features
and hails from the same species
he has our smile and creeds
and pathology of the soul
and the greed for vanity's sake.

He's different the experts say
but not that much from the Enabler,
he is illogical says the Dialectician
and insane concludes the Psychiatrist
but not that much from the Mother Cell
the nourishing source
the germinating seed
the empty space here and there
even within the friendly enclosure
the furtive look of the neighbor
the effort to avoid all contact.
the empty square
seriality at the neighborhood level
like I saw it in the South End.

He is the apple fallen near the tree
the product of the chemical mix;
he is NRA, the Congress and Wall Street's
combined voracity just like *larrons en foire*
to create Makabral and Maldyòk.

He is you and I assembled
in automation made fate
and faith in the Market's goodness
in the gun's good feeling
and its mythologized lore
the Second Amendment made fetish
of a nation guided by high valued imperatives

of the Military Industrial Technological Complex
and desensitized by mediated hypes
by the Nintendo's procurement of pleasure to kill
the thrill of the murderous instinct
the lost spirits already perturbed
would find solace in madness
a shorter distance to salvation.

No! He is not the Other, the killer,
he is not even a stranger
he is part of a whole
prototype of a rational scenario
perhaps your existential denial.

The little fan of the New York Yankees
who refused to leave home and yet
still was getting the excitement rolling
in the schoolyard and beyond;
the little beautiful darling, smart light
and pride of her parents;
they had not had the time
nor to have or to inspire hatred;
they didn't ask to come among us
still they took pleasure and reveled
in the happening of the moment
in the miracle of growing and learning.

"We cannot go back to the school,"
they said, "we don't have a teacher anymore."
Other teachers are trapped before death
and yet still trying to save their pupils' lives;
parents who will never see them
their memories haunted by every instant
that preceded the fateful morning.

The most evil emblem after all
despite images of gunman toting gun
is the quiet of corporate input analysis,
the invisibility of arms-profiting dividends

   In the Beast's Alley (Poems of conscience)

the big guy that pockets the plus-value
from killings and mayhems
from families in pain;
the honorable entrepreneur hero
who produces a high-tech producing factory
that produces the AR-15 style rifle
and the elegant, sky-lurking drones
that kill thousands of miles away in the comfort
of the peaceful father in a US suburb
in the invisibility of the distance.

They hire MIT geniuses for maximum effect
those kill as magicians do
to erase all links to physicality
as if God himself had conducted the action,
metacosmic fluidity guided by laser,
and yet the blood spilled is real,
real red blood of the villagers;
they kill, the drones, with an impunity
more impenetrable than the Newtown killings
those have never paid for their deeds
because no deed was ever committed
in the absence of accountability.

Killing is never justified
although it always has a context
even a nourishing matrix
and a bad attitude
and a huge arsenal of means.

Even Halliburton which sells arms
and oil and illusions and cynicism
in the same package is innocent in this scheme:
the soul of the country wants it, they say,
the Founding Fathers wanted it, they say,
major national interests want it, they say,
it's the continuation of the fairy tale.

They kill for the Empire
as for the nation-state
for the honor of the family
for the decimals on the bank account;
they kill because they have the means,
beautiful garments for social engineering.

Before all the tears will have dried off
and the spotlight changes focus
and the next mayhem occurs
and the memories of the twenty-six
evaporate in the air and Walmart registers
its nice cut in weapon sale
and the maniac gets to be happy
with his beautiful dispenser of horrors
and the mayor gets to show magnanimity
confronting a danger minutes after the fact
and the Guns Producer Industrial Complex
shows robust elevated patterns
and the Psychologist shows, immovable,
confirmed tendency to deviance,
hate of the mother and her doubles
and the children, product of her matrix:
casualties of madness
also of living cost challenges
innocence perished in Hell,
that's what these children are
in the objective meanness of Globality.

They are not rare artistic marvels
for the sake of beauty, the weapons,
they are instrument to an aim
regardless of the original intent;
their function is to kill
and ease up the labor of God
manifested in sport killing
in political killing

    In the Beast's Alley (Poems of conscience)

in Mafia killing
in killing for the pleasure of the libido
testosterone in *chute libre.*

I invite you, my friend,
to stroll along the river way
on a full moon any night
when a warm, caressing wind penetrates
the instant, oh eternal instant!
I invite you to join in and rejoice
of the splendor of the space, its smell,
I invite you to let loose
of all the links of horrors
and the false stress
and the appetite for hideous thrills.

Before Newtown there was Oklahoma City
there were Kent State, Waco and Colorado
there were Wounded Knee and the Négrier
there were My Lai, Abu Ghraib and Fallujah
there were Hiroshima and Nagasaki
there were LaSalin and Site Solèy
all memories of past thrills.

(The children would not have died in vain
if we approach thoroughly the calamity
and its many facets; often the absurd is the problem
that has eluded conscience's penetrating gaze.)
These little cadavers conjure you to close down
both the engines and the sustaining source of Hell;
they conjure you to sanity's road in the face
of madness and cold-blooded interests;
they conjure you to utopia
they conjure you to elevation of the senses.

      (Boston, January 2013)

The Children of Bin Laden Didn't Know

The children didn't know
the tall man was wanted
they didn't know their mother
was harboring terrorists on the run
they didn't know you can kill a man
without a warrant nor even a word
they didn't know you can kill
while they're still at sleep.

The children didn't know
prior on a nine-eleven on a single morning
three thousands people were murdered
like birds caged on a hellish summer day
they didn't know you can kill
per order of a Declaration
per order of a religious book
per order of the president even when
the country's laws say No.

The children didn't know the death
of five people can be celebrated
along the boulevard in daylight.
The children didn't know
tall pappy was wanted for murders
they didn't know they were
targets of Drones and special SEALs
they didn't know there was a price
on their families' head and fate.

They didn't know you can be civilized
and kill other humans without a warrant
they didn't know you can make
your own international code of law
they didn't know that power can explain
everything and respect not even a token rule
they didn't know that the most powerful's reason

 In the Beast's Alley (Poems of conscience)

is always the best to follow if you're sane
they didn't know humans sometimes are insane
they didn't' know you can be this and not that.

The children didn't know tall pappy was facing
a 350-million strong unique superpower
they didn't know he was both a villain and hero.

They didn't know if you can get a Drone
and three dozens of SEALs and a huge megaphone
and the homogeneous tone of Media and Nation
and the holly, bully pulpit of a charming president
you can make killing look like a nice thing
even justice on Earth and joy to the people.
You can even invent a new perfect nation.
The children didn't know any of that.

(May 2011)

The Siege and the Killings in Homs, Houla, Hama (Syria)

*(this poem is dedicated to the unrelenting
resistance of the Syrian people against State
oppression despite murderous carnage)*

A Macabre indecency
a systematic barrage of fire
symmetric even in horror
cast a specter of death
all over the city, maiming and killing
from the sure distance of power
power of the artillery
power of the State
power of State immunity.

Removing the world's agenda venom
against everything Syrian-like,
this *Boston Globe's* article speaks volumes:
*"During a terrifying two minutes…
At least 22 bodies, including that of 6-year-old
Mohammad Yahia Al-Wees were recovered…
And amid the rubble on the stairway of the
ground floor, 10 yards from the door and possibly
safety, lay the bodies of two foreign journalists,
Marie Colvin, and Remi Achilk…"*

A macabre indecency,
but an irony of fate and history
that the Romans' wretched,
the terrorist of time past,
special guest villain in Others-haters' show
and in the warmongers' holy book
that includes offspring of Saladin and of Genghis Khan,
offspring of Toussaint and the shoeless fighters
is now killing his own in *cold bloody* indifference…

    In the Beast's Alley (Poems of conscience)

Conscience doesn't discriminate
even when petrified by terror and madness,
even when horrified by fear of the unknown,
fear of the uncertainties of finitude;
fear of the *cafard*, the blues,
the blue blues of *Makabral*;
fear of saying the impolitely
correct thing that disturbs the gentry
instead of seeking clarity.
Still conscience doesn't let fear
silence her forever.

What's wrong with calling for freedom
says this father whose two sons were slaughtered
early in the morning without much warning:
Freedom for the people! Freedom of conscience!
he says even though for his sons it was too late.

Conscience must not discriminate
regardless the manner the killing was performed
be it done by drones on your family villages away
or on your neighbor next door in large urban centers
like in Homs and Houla in the heart of Syria
where kids were massacred like toads
just the same the indignation should be.
Killing must not be an option
especially for the most powerful State;
it should be *in jure* or *de facto*
the never acceptable mischief…

On a certain Wednesday of hell
More than 40 women and children were among
78 killed in Mazraat al-Qubeir, near Hama,
killed by remote barrage of the artillery;
those killings from the sure distance of power
power of the blunt interests of the State's minions
power of immunity of the Syrian army

—must now cease and desist.
The people of Homs and Houla and Hama must live
free!

(June 2012)

 In the Beast's Alley (Poems of conscience)

What Resilience Ain't

It shouldn't be resignation
nor Idontgiveitdamness
of the soul and the mind;
it shouldn't be devotion
to the shallowest of ideas
of those connected to the mundanity
and to the crass impulse of the flesh
inhibiting the sound judgment
even of the wisest of the sages.

It shouldn't be the ditching
to survival's black hole
of your most sacred values
only to delay for one day
the inevitability of what should be.

It shouldn't be masochism
of self-hated victims of oppression
giving up the struggle for freedom
to secure a less unpredictable fate.

It should not be delegation
to the most idiotic among us
or to Wall Street's greediest ethos
of our right to a dignified life.

It shouldn't be accommodation
to nature's maddening onslaught hidden
under the guise of faith, law and order
while the culprit is closer to home.

It shouldn't be accepting intolerance
and inequality and an unjust order
and what you're told since childhood
as being reality and cosmic destiny.

It shouldn't be that
but rather this
rather the other side of the Universe
the unknown multitude lost in banality
and in the indifference of absence.

Rather the engagement in the Absurd
than the myopia of the perception;
rather the feeling of the pain
and the glory of the last hurrah
than the pathetic robot's state;
rather the phoenix's metamorphosis
than the unending torpor-like routine
rather the resistance to finitude
than the boredom of the same-old-thing.

It shouldn't be habituation
to the conditioning of the senses
nor the appeasement of the libido
by the Behavior Control Department.

Resilience should not be atonement
nor penitence for imaginary sins;
it's the re-hurrah of the last hurrah
it's the zombie tasting salt
despite the master's objection *
it's the wretched conquering the Temple
it's the beauty of the poetic word
the elegance of the liberated zest
the magic of the love song
the everlasting conquest of the beast
by the simple majesty of art and folly.

* In Haitian mythology a zombie will regain conscious-
ness if he/she tastes salt.

    (April 2012)

        In the Beast's Alley (Poems of conscience)

Rebel Perimeter

(dedicated to the Occupy Wall Street protesters)

Rebel perimeter
or refuge for the drunks
the kids' first night out
the depressed, lonely heart.

The People's Republik
even Che Guevara's picture
and realist-socialist posters
and neo-realist paintings of locals
and poets writing while drinking,
and noisy out-of-state students
suddenly feeling an air of freedom
after too many extra drinks;
the repository of the town's soul,
its weaknesses and its dreams,
its fantasy, its *dépravés*,
all played their roles
in the making of the nightmare
in the making of misery
in the making of the zombie state
exonerating Wall Street
its thievery
its bubbles
its suddenly becoming rich bastards
its fabulously and magically generated
riches on a piece of paper
or a computer screen;
its blaming of the poor
or the teenage mother;
its blaming of the welfare state,
of "Obamacare"
and the "stimulus plan,"
of happy-spender-democrats

who joined them as two-faced medal
in the blaming of the immigrants
forgetting they have heartily saved
the country from boredom;
its hatred of the Other
its suffocating of the others
its diabolical management of life
its insensibility to human pain
its profit-before-anything-else ethos
its I-don't-give-it-damn dogma
its bombing of Libya on a whim
its speculation on oil price
its privatization of jail
its privatization of health
its privatization of love,
they all participate
in the building of hell
and its corollaries
and its false splendor.

Rebel perimeter
space to let it be
or wait until Human again
becomes a mystery,
until greater search is made to secure
a sustaining breathing space
or until the robotic, twisted Unsoul
has managed to impose universal control
in the Greater Order of Things
through power pattern
and data selection
and gerrymandering
or voters' suppression
or military coup d'état in banana republic
with CIA sponsorship
and Big Brother's good advice

　　　　In the Beast's Alley (Poems of conscience)

and Big Business complicity
and Big Brother looking
while the inside of the soul is missing.

Rebel perimeter
or lacking of wisdom
or betting on surrendering
to the easier way out of madness.

Rebel perimeter,
wait when you no longer accept
for conscience such a pitiful role
and see follow the Contingence Void
the apprehension of appearance's foolishness
and the selling of the soul to Unsoul,
and the collapse of the Stock Market
and the belated understanding of poetry
as both epiphany and redemption.

The last hour never rang
before fate has put its stamps
before the water starts boiling,
that's the day of the reckoning
the deceased's revival day,
day of beauty on Earth.

The Brooklyn Bridge is closed
occupied by those who have had enough
just like before them the angry Haitians
who said Hell with racist exclusion;
yes, Occupy Wall Street,
that's the cry of conscience
—and intelligence.

(October 2011)

Simbi in the Water*

Caressed by the slow, cool wind
on a Sunny Sunday in the Caribbean Fall
rejuvenated
invigorated
bursting from elation of being
along the beach's quiet wave
amorously blinded by Simbi's lovely gaze
love at first sight:
You will never be seen again
on Earth or anywhere;
Simbi's charm has conquered
in a swift, mysterious, and deft move
both your body and your soul
now evaporated in the eerie world
she is taking charge of all your emotions
mistress of your space and time.

You are being retaken by Simbi
new returnee to the Ether world
carried deep inside the ocean's matrix
Simbi is now your only friend
your *nanm*, your spirit is left behind **.
you are the waters' guest
prisoner from the past world
you are the new guest of Agwe ***
the inheritor of the mantra
in deep, sub-oceanic Black Hole
the spirits traveling at human pace.

Simbi-in-the-Water
elegant, majestic, beautiful
rarely strikes in someone's lifetime
then when the bell rings often out of the blue
in whirlwind occurrence the sacrifice must be total
new way of being must be invented

                    In the Beast's Alley (Poems of conscience)

a new sub-oceanic consciousness
has now made the rounds of our humankind
Agwe and Simbi and Humans
together sharing forbidden lost space
in the ocean's depth, enjoying life's vibes
and joining together to create new energy,
new elation, creation, cosmic renewal,
water and carbon forming the essence,
primal causality of being
the unveiling of the mystery
the revealing of what should be.

    (November 2010)

* Simbi-in the-Water means *Simbi-nan-dlo* in Haitian; it
refers to Simbi, the Vodou god of sea, water, singing, who
lives in deep water. This poem was first published in the
anthology *Ocean Voices,* edited by Everett Hoagland, ed.
Spinner Publications, New Bedford, Massachusetts, 2013.
** *Nanm* means spirit, consciousness, cognitive faculty
in Haitian Creole.
*** *Agwe* is another Vodou god of the sea, and also of
travel, exile.

The People Cannot Wait For Godot

*(to honor the second anniversary of the
earthquake, an anniversary of hurt, neglect,
solidarity, resistance, and hope)*

The people cannot wait for Godot
nor for you to secure the seashore
and close off the airports
for relief to arrive.

They cannot wait
until donors resolve their differences
over the proper way to disburse
money not too long ago promised
right hand flatly placed on the heart.

They cannot wait
until your agenda is advanced
amid vast lands of suffering;
they cannot wait
until the bureaucrats are comfortable
with grandiosely laid numerical data
for the first tents to be given.

They cannot wait
for the birds to return
from a long journey of absence
nor until the rain will have impregnated
the lake through the soil's porous leak.

They didn't wait, indeed,
instead put their own hands
fighting rubble after rubble
colossal endeavor for many
sometimes by total strangers
to rescue people from sure death.

     In the Beast's Alley (Poems of conscience)

They didn't wait, indeed
they brought food and water
to their brethrens from villages away;
they didn't wait for Godot to arrive
indeed they were the only rescuers
months after goudougoudou's onslaught
with a cholera epidemic as dessert
and Baby Doc's return as nightmare.

They didn't wait to be there,
even when they wholeheartedly
welcomed the beautiful human embrace
to save lives and honor the living
the universal longing
to bring humanity's horrors
to conscience's acute gaze
the survivors' smile
being their strategic weapon.

The people didn't wait for Godot
to erect beauty amid the rubble
through colors and testimonials,
through the poetry of solidarity
through artisticalisation of experience
through rendering and retelling and
re-apprehending the parts lost in the
common pits, the extra-dimension,
the sympathy of the senses, huge leap
to regain possession of their souls,
to reinvent the dimension of hope
and see how long patience will endure.

They have regained possession
through their own idea of the self
of the integrity of their dignity
making suffering and crying in a hole
a vast human project cast in universal glory,

fusion with the Other and with others,
space, the earth renewed in colors,
yes, colors, colors of the beast,
colors of goudougoudou,
colors of Jacmel,
its mountains,
its shore.

Haiti is family
she is today suffering stoically,
in the silence broken by the breeze;
Haiti is family,
mother of Latin America,
the magical maker of our modernity
the voice of alterity,
the voice of the lost tribe
the incarnation of the beauty of black
the place where surrealism married
magical realism under a coconut tree.

Haiti, the sinner for the West's gentry
and for the Christian right,
dance, light, music in the funeral!

Haiti is your phantasm
the island that makes love with its gods
universal human project
baptismal font for greed
and for human covenant to save decency
great universal for alienation and yet
unmediatized by fear nor avarice.

The people did not wait for Godot, we say,
they are the apostles of the here and now
they rally together to stop the river of tears.

A new dawn was made from the rubble,
thousands colors of light, life renewal,

In the Beast's Alley (Poems of conscience)

have replaced nature's maddening onslaught,
companions from earth's mysterious conscience
have joined the great constellation of beauty,
the people will have survived, proud people,
they will have survived for another eternity.

(2010)

Motion*

*(a poem I thought of while walking to my job
along Webster Avenue-Columbia Street line)*

Voum! Voum! Voum!
The walker slows down
feeling now handicapped
by the harried drivers.

The morning is soothed,
ordinary morning
in ordinary time
by a slowly moving breeze
and a chorus of horns.

The streets are invaded,
clogged from east to west,
bloated through south and north
by a cohort of metallic *gibiers.*

Jumping like a limping duke
revealing contingence
I reflect on the innocence
on the grand irony of fate,
the Church on the corner right
apartment building on the left
the flock are all present.

At the Bottle & Can Return
two redeemers are waiting, ready
to collect the meal of the day,
the company as happily
on top of revenues from parts
of cars squeezed like sardines
has added to its chest this extra:
ecolos, pathos and Adam Smith
on the same winning team.

   In the Beast's Alley (Poems of conscience)

This one frequents the library
which he makes his domain,
I'm always wondering whether
he is lazy, freaky, crazy,
or all three alchemicized
in the pleasure of living
and defying expectations.

Next to the four-corner of hell
comes the treacherous street
with the nice policeman policing
the traffic with warming smile;
he has seen it all he's saying.

The young man seems on top
of the world and his dreams,
in the cell phone he holds lies
the proof of raising illusions;
a few blocks down to the cars'zone
emerge three perfectly attired
brothers in a dark car, hoods
placed over their heads, smoking
just like in the Steel Pulse song,
perfectly fitting the profile,
the Trayvon Martin prototype.
Kids from the nearby high school
on an impressive ride, chilling.

The train! I had forgotten it
until like a hurried boa
it sneaked out of the tunnel
under my unsure feet deciding
whether to back up or speed up
as the train's silhouette faded away.

The motion created
in void, in the law of movement
a dynamic instant.

The traffic never stopped
the routine of life flowing
and again and again
the universe in motion.

Low on inspiration and tricks
I resorted to the Cosmos
and its action and creation
as I applauded the Higgs's boson
discovery after so many years of faith;
it's like phenomenology
thought through infinitesimal
possibilities and goals of,
the Thing becoming us
and us them like Spinoza
thought it, like poets always do,
senses and imagination.

Voum! Voum! Voum!
The journey changes to routine
the space and even the motion
become my intimate milieu;
the moment passes in times
the souvenir will remain forever
even long after evanescence creeps in.

* First published in the journal *Auscultations*, June 2013.

   In the Beast's Alley (Poems of conscience)

When Memo Came

And blizzard Memo came
vengeful for letting us enjoy
two years of a normal winter
in usual erratic New England fashion.
Even no non-sense Union Square, hectic
in any given day has gained some allure,
the roof of Saint Joseph Church became
the instant of a frightful snow storm
a Roman column ready to vanquish the enemy
and the pigeons stood guard, valorous gladiators,
in military row displaying the glory of Memo.
Behind piles of still brightening snow, part dirty
and unappealing, part untouched by human labor
even in high unemployment time, came Fredo,
his face has mimicked the darkness of the night,
half sleeping and disturbed by the awakening day:
where had he been, Fredo? He had survived,
atlas, he had survived Memo's wrath.

An Autumn Night

The autumn night brings
the unsettling transition to new,
cold breezes invading the senses
in calming accompaniment of the music
coming from the O'Brian Pub's window
smoothing away whatever pain there was.

The autumn night's vibes
and its melodious energy filtered
through its violent cadency and rhythm
endeared the new season with celestial charm
even amid serial insignificance and gloom.

The autumn night brings joy
and affirms our existence's connection
to others and to the search for grace
and to the reach of *complétude*
and to Johnny Cash's singing our universality
and everyday themes of living and making love
near a flowing creek alongside the quiet road.

   In the Beast's Alley (Poems of conscience)

For You Whose Name I Don't Know

They are nice those passing,
Furtive moments lasting seconds
I take delight of your smile
And savor your perfume in distance.

The next time I'll tell you about
Treasures buried outside naked views,
Flowers waiting to spread for the spring,
The great feast on the way to Nirvana.

Sensations suffice to please me
In the instant if only your eyes
Stay beaming the way I love them
And make it a continuing present.
You don't have a name perhaps
Not even corporal existence.

(December 2009)

In the Beast's Alley (Poems of conscience)

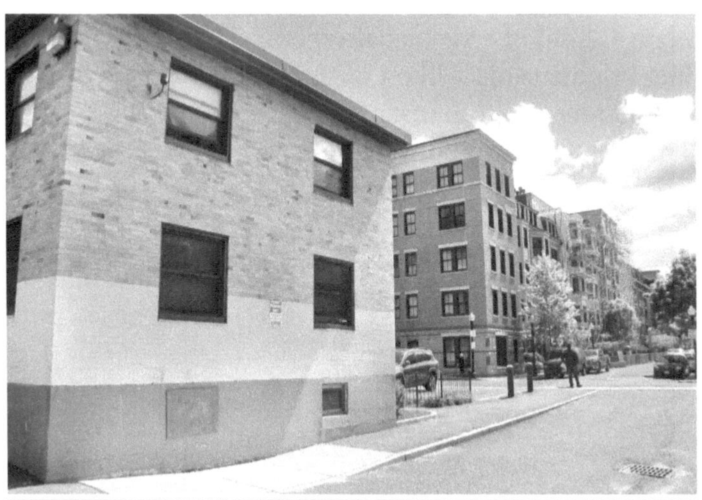

A view of the two worlds in Boston —*photo by Patrick Sylvain, 2013.*

If She Would Be Rimbaud's Shrink

He would conquer the oceans
And the immense continents
And the hearts of the mountains
Even the matrix of infinity.

If she would be Rimbaud's shrink
He would avoid Hell's fate
He would recreate new spaces
Smile and beauty will unite.

He was kind of eerie that afternoon
Her brightened face like a *sursis*
Would save life in an instant
That the dying would want be eternal.

Except that she is infinity.

(March 2010)

April Fool: He Saw Her Again, He Said

Again, in a passing moment
and again he saw her
furtively his eyes brightened
in the immensity of the joy.

He hopes of a secret
tunneling their inner desire
would meet unhindered
by the temperance of inadvertence
nor by ordinary happenstance.
To himself he murmured:
May one day I see her outside time,
has she always known this?
Then he realized he was just dreaming.
A day dream.

(April 2010)

I cry for all madness' dead

(or the correlation of terror)

You will have it
and then nothing
you will enjoy it
and then tired of it
you will return
to time's boredom
even the thrill
of killing and gaining
and being adulated
by abused dumb
won't last for long.

The mom's en route
to her child's madrasa
and the lone London serviceman
and the Palestinian in Gaza
and the Boston Marathon lovers
share the same horrible fate;
they are not wannebe fedayin
but the IDF kids don't play game
neither the Pentagon or Élysée
neither the crazy unemployed dude
victim of exclusion
witness to horror
neither the pain-stricken orphan
enchanted by the fiery imam
neither the rejected
dejected of his dream.
I cry for all madness' dead.

(May 2013)

     In the Beast's Alley (Poems of conscience)

Boston's Gripping Charm

Boston laments I

*(dedicated to the bombing victims of the
Boston Marathon on April 15, 2013)*

They reenacted Athens's grandeur
and made the athletes run distances;
they ran just for the fun of running
the well-endowed as well as the crippled
to ease up contingence and void.

The mountains invited to silence
even in the middle of terror
the ascending thrill was like orgasm
elevated but died in its *plénitude.*

It was a brilliant day for running
the people came to the rendez-vous
as loyal fans paying a debt of love;
Martin came his young soul full of joy
it's the moment of embrace for beauty.

The victims shared the space
with the creator of their agony
in fateful relaxation and smile
running is energy in motion
athletic endeavor to adjust
to the infinity rhythm.

Killing refuses to others their dues
in the negotiation over space and time
always it should be defensive if one vows
to stay part of a civilized human tribe;
the killers mimicked others' indifference
to the people's anguish when it is not theirs;
it's the spiral of the tormented reproducing

torment and tears on a smaller scale.
I cried for a too young a life lost
as sacrificial lamb in Empire's game
and as casualty to alienation's harm
killing for a book or for an injustice
doesn't fix the problem of madness and greed.

It has hit home to me the terror in the heart
of Boston the bombers living as eerie it could be
a few blocks down my street and smoking pot
in alleys; the lockdown like a Latin-American coup
blocked my movement and I became prisoner of
terrorist hysteria and hype in media age
and enlightened by patriotic act and control.

Little Martin, and Krystle, Lu and Sean*
couldn't script their fate the worst that day,
a spring and sunny day, welcoming the runners.
The two brothers have shamed
and the land and its imagery
say those who couldn't fathom
rare species from blurry space
the meaning of it all
the meaning of a non-sense
visible only to the blind.

Crying, yes, I cry for your dead
what about the others, the unseen ones?
I cry for the schoolboy on the bus, his ash
amassed silently by his mourning mother,
blown up from the Earth by pure reenactment
of evil deeds done not too long ago
dreadful misunderstanding
a pretext to a curse
a testimony to absurdity.

They die by false duty-bound sense
they die for your honor and a verse

　　In the Beast's Alley (Poems of conscience)

interpreted for operative deeds and goals;
or for the privileges of the few blessed ones
holding the projection of Empire's Global Design;
most don't care anyway it could as well be the moon
or transcendence's thrill or whatever else
for it's not a business to be bothered with.

Hitler's concentration camps and his hellish legacy
brilliant agents of hell as it could be are now made
museum thrills and curiosity pleasers all over
for happy duty-free tourists with enough cash to spare,
Boston Copley Square will be next
the industry has never lost a dime,
the lesson is nor learned—however.

The blood is of the same substance,
and the tears colorless as the rain,
the London killers' hands were red
so is the blood shed by the drones,
same is the murmur of suffering
of all affected by such an horrible deed.

Killing is personal for the marathoners
as for their fans who lined up the streets
on a sunny, cool and brightening Monday
not knowing in seconds their bodies and souls
would be thrown to Gehenna's abyss;
still the horror could not kill the people's
marvelous union and communal aim to stay put
—strong Boston remains even in pain.

(May 2013)

* First names of the victims killed in the Boston Marathon
bombings and in the subsequent MIT attack allegedly
perpetrated by the brothers Dzhokhar and Tamerlan
Tsaraev.

In the Beast's Alley (Poems of conscience)

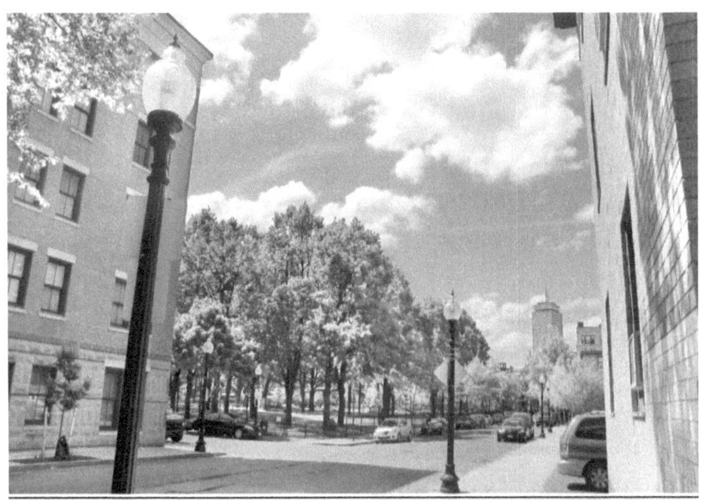

Another view of the two worlds in Boston —*photo by Patrick Sylvain, 2013.*

The Place Where They Go

(Boston laments II)

The place where they go
to blow up tall buildings
with daring coldbloodness
and making a mockery of the
suffering and the broken hearts
and the fear to go down the street
giving to skinheads their glory
under the brilliant sun and the reps
and lobbies in Congress their Patriot Act II.

The place where they go
to school and learn ignorance
from the most prestigious of teachers
and the faith in killing at the church
and the mistrust of the neighbors and
rivalry with friends and mentors
even when all is well in the paradise.

The place where they go
to acquire knowledge and know-hows
to build bombs and blow up Marathoners
on a sunny Monday in a Boston street
and to learn to relax while others are in tears
and to have whole cities applaud their policemen
for barricading them as goody-goody sheep.

The place where they go
to kill children while in school and cry
crocodile tears until the next mayhem
and the tormented gets his thrill and the NRA
garnishes its rating and the arm industry its values
and the patriot his Second amendment safe
and all has returned to normal and business as usual.

    In the Beast's Alley (Poems of conscience)

The place where they go to learn
as a Vodou bòkò's magic to kill sitting
a world away in a nice office chair
the thrill blinding the flow of the blood on the hut's floor
and the sound of the cries of sudden orphans bewildered
and stricken in pain and thinking of revenge and all.

The place where they go could be anywhere that offers
solace and praise for the most robotic among us and sell
the unimaginable to happy zombies in the name of Allah
and to non-believers that don't give it shit either way.

The place where they go is a state of the mind conceived
by years endured in hardship in the beast's alleys and
survived as if awakening from a long acid trip and never
got to know whether the journey was worth the effort
or the effort worthy of such a great journey.

The place where they go
just to go away
and rebuild the mind with new nutrients
defying the law of grandeur and greed;
the place where they go
to reimagine what could be
and make a vow to defeat
all that which magnifies madness
the place where they go
to clear up their minds.

The place where they go
to blow up happy faces
and false innocence
and the hypocritical ethicals
and all that which breathes and dreams
even their own want
even the possibility of rebirth.

The place where they go
to seek refuge and calm
is the place they bomb
regardless of the sorrow
they cause to avenge other dead;
the place where they go
to avoid horrifying Russian missiles
and Pentagon drones and all
is the place they bomb on Patriot Day.

(May 2013)

I see coming the ghost

*(Boston laments III / Dedicated to Patrick Sylvain /
About the process of gentrification that has taken
place along the Washington Street and Harrison
Avenue corridor in the Boston South End)*

I see coming the ghost
of a past life seen only in photos
the uprooting of souvenirs
of those who have made it their homes,
tossing the baby along with the shovel.

I see the two parallel universes
no longer care even for the pretense
of letting the island of hopelessness
be redeemed in the same space,
the Cathedral being only a specter
God and Capital united.

I see coming the ghost
of the Franklin Street Park's
neglected beauty like a misty morning
in an impressionist painting turned
to inaccessible and forbidden land.
I see coming the ghost
of my brother's lonely rest
under the big tree's bench
the silhouette of the Prudential
casting its bright shadow
as big brother's hidden eyes
on the whole neighborhood.

I see coming the ghost
looking at the well-crafted scaffold
and the stark modernization placard
planted by Boston Housing Authority
boasting camera surveillance as added quality

and eco-green as supportive endorsement
and the face-lifted and over-beautified park
and the dramatically lighted furniture stores
and the Japanese restaurant with sushi
that along will come the silent suffering.

I see coming the ghost
and the silent suffering but who cares
if the land of plenty has enough grains
for the errand birds and the kids
whether the space cannot be owned
whether hopelessness has a place to live?

I see coming the ghost
of past successful development
seen elsewhere on this land
the harbinger of what will be
the wiping out of undesirables
the victory over bad taste and bad choice
urban chic at its best.

I see coming the ghost
of the displaced to the fear zone
instability and morosity and
hindrance-provoking energy flew
toward nothingness and boredom.

I see coming the ghost
of plenitude in absence as a curse;
it's a systematic Grand Design of
money-making machines, ingenuity,
collateral damage is the price to pay.
The logic is the essence, they say, soulless
epigrowth, impermeable to all value systems.

Still I mourn the passing to distant memory
of the long, creep-inducing boulevard
the mystery of danger and the feel of bravura
in darkness and owe of fantasized zest.

                    In the Beast's Alley (Poems of conscience)

I see coming the ghost
of a Boston returned to the gentry's lore
without the mask of bourgeois Janus's faith
enlightened breed chanting equality and all
while making sure inequality is the rule.

I see coming the ghost
as I survey the sudden cleanliness
and majesty of streets and baby carriers
and the dogs' special park and care
and the health food joint and the gym
of a brain new place I never knew.

(Boston, May 2013)

Big Brother Is Watching

(dedicated to Edward Snowden and Julian Assange)
"the public needs to know the kinds of things a
government does in its name, or the "consent
of the governed" is meaningless."

   —Edward Snowden

Watch out! they say
Big Brother is watching!
Watch out! they say
The magnifier is on.

Watch out! they say
Don't make it too easy
For the Shadow Angel
To select his prey.

Watch out! they say
The Panopticon is creepier
And way out of way
Than you were left to know.

Watch out! they say
What they say they'd do
They do it and more
To make sure Hell is well.

Watch out! they say
You are the catched fish
And Facebook and Yahoo
And Google are your trap.

Watch out! they say
We are not the enemies
Remember Daniel Ellsberg
And all the lies after.

     In the Beast's Alley (Poems of conscience)

Watch out! they say
The choice is yours and ours
It could be village
Or an Hobbesian Whole.

The Teen and the Sharkish Gaze

*(dedicated to Trayvon Martin cowardly murdered
by George Zimmerman in Sanford, Florida, on
the night of February 26, 2012; a crime for which
Zimmerman was eventually found not guilty
by a six-female, almost all white jury. Major
protests erupted in many US cities demanding
that the Justice Department press civil rights
violation charges against Zimmerman)*

It was a pre-spring in the rain
the soil soaked in the silence
of the dark night and the sharkish gaze
of a vigilante with malady-stricken thought
and aim of salvation and protection and insulation
of the coveted false paradise
false sense of menace and lacking
the nightmare of invading hordes
the boredom of unalterable emptiness
and family dysfunction, living absurdity
amid law and order and disorder
and laissez-faire economics mixed
with the Far-West attitude
and habitude of conqueror
the Big White Complex of old
Jim Crow in the remaking
remixed for twenty-first century taste
Tea Party and NRA working in unison
toward a USA without the Other.

And the teen in the slow pace walking
his hoodie as profiled-thuggish thief enveloped
his innocent head while his hands hold Skittles candy
and juice, hurrying to escape; he's scared
of the penetrating gaze, the evolving horror

but he stands heroic to the price of his life
defying the accusing gaze of madness
projected as a vast fishing net;
the mapping of the coveted enclosure,
the Rousseauian founder of social order
claiming ownership of empty space
and building dreams of grandeur and greed
this time it is not even his to take;
he is pure illusion, the eager stalker,
but he has a gun and a sickened flair
the teen has no chance and even his innocence
cannot spare him since other forces are at play:
Only the roaring of revolt may save the day,
and one hundred cities-strong,
a people's tsunami upholds the ideal
even the lynchings cannot destroy,
even the beating of Rodney King cannot uproot,
even the killing of Amadou Diallo cannot sully.

He had the right to be there
and not be dead for a curse
a teen looking for his better days
as we all do before our prime;
it's pity after such a long trail
that we should fail to pursue the right rail
the search for beauty remains the best moral grail
even when all seems so deleteriously baneful.

It's not even about him, the eager stalker,
nor about the hand that acted on that night;
it's about deeds that took place five thousands years ago
in many continents; it's not about the symptoms
it lies in deeper roots and deeper entrenchment,
deeper perversion of the ideal of being
it lays at its Trans-Atlantic foundational scheme,
in the trade and the plantation's hell.

In the silence of the dark night
and soil soaked by the pre-spring rain
the lurking, eager stalker got his prey,
the president got his *bon mot*
he can honor his neutral aura
while Jim Crow returns as the law
of the land, sneaky law and low imposition
of charm and malignity, the gun lobby perseveres
demanding its dues as noblesse oblige
while a whole race is subjected to hatred
to the infamy of less than human value,
this is America the beautiful;
Cornell West says POTUS is the global lurking gaze
tossing drones and tears on unaware villagers
whose families are falling dead like birds.

It's about the shallow rationale that makes
British royal babies and O.J. relevant;
the logic of dummies and dupes and doped,
the pre-ordained conditioning of a young man
willing to help sustain the illusion of Having,
the buying of a fake state of being
the lunatic avenger of the white pride
like the zealous policeman thinks he's saving the State;
alienation comes in different shades and shapes.
You may kill, my friend, in a pre-spring night
still your salvation is far a good done deal,
you better find a better way for a change;
luckily the 100-city protests set a different tone:
We are still dreaming of a new dawn.

      —Tontongi, July 2013

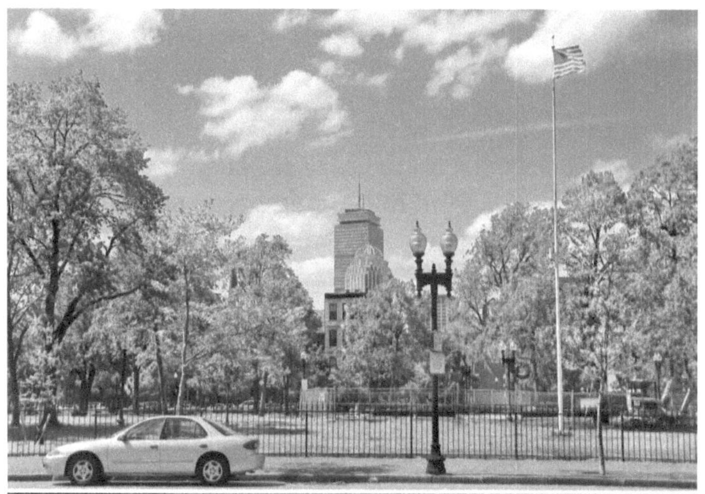

A view of the Franklin Street Park, the Prudential Building is seen in the background —*photo by Patrick Sylvain, 2013.*

Four Poems Translated in Haitian Creole

Dlo n'ap bwè k'ap nwaye n*

*(Èg la ak kòk la ap ponpe)**

Èg la deplwaye zèl li alavironnbadè, elegan, kè kontan ;
Bèk li ba l anbisyon pou l konkeri latè san remò ni regrè.
Grandizè satisfè ki konn ki bezwen ki fè l pran gran chimen
Pèp la te asepte laperèz, malalèz, makakri kè tounen san koule
E menm malediksyon pou l te ka selebre yon sèl jou libere.

Peyi a te bèl ak koulè wouj pou san ak lespwa,
Ak koulè ble tristès, koulè konsyans lavi.
Peyi a te bèl tou ak ven mil ti lanj gadyen marin
Ki te pot pwoteksyon grann pwisans kontrolè.
Moun ak mòn yo te bèl, bèl te bèl baboukèt !

Prezidan an te tounen kè kontan selebre toupatou,
Se te demand pèp la sou yon rejim sanwont, kokinè
Ki t'ap dekonstonbre lavi e dechire lalin, bloke lapli,
Fanm ak fanmi vyole, timoun san manje, dlo nan je.
Veye yo ! Veye yo ! An n kontinye baleye lakou a !

Vakabon ak makout se nich gèp ak dyondyon,
Yo leve toupatou, nan kazèn koulè jonn krazezo
Kou nan biwo klimatize zotobre eksplwatè.
Yo la tou nan rapò ak data fichye Depatman Deta
E sou yon tèt dola vèt kou yon medsin anmè.

Konpè m vin sèl bèt nan lakou k'ap chante bèl lomaj
Pou fòs batayon l yo ak bèl ti souri sou lèv li. *Happy !*
Zèv li tou vin yon lwanj pou l selebre viktwa inivèsèl
Nan yon mond zonbifye k ap chache goute sèl je klere !
Mond moun gounanbouch, moun vant plen ak lespwa.

    In the Beast's Alley (Poems of conscience)

Moun vivan jwenn grandè yo nan libète total.
Libète ak bèlte, jwisans lavi, lanmò, lanmou
Se sous desten tout moun k ap viv santiman yo
Nan yon teren pyeje, yon tèt-chaje kont-mal-taye,
Oh ! Moun yo mande jistis yo fin ase soufwi !

Oh ! Mwen pè pou yo pa tronpe w ankò, o gran pèp !
Gran vanyan lejandè ki te fann vant kolon atoufè ;
Pèp ki te brile latè menm pou l refize desten bèkèkè,
Ki jodia ap vale yon remèd anmè pou zonbi desale.
Veye yo ! Veye yo ! siveye vòlè yo nan tanp la !

Sa fè m mal nan kè m e nan kò m pi mal ke oun maladi,
Sa fè mwen vle vomi, sa wonje sansiblite nanm mwen
Lè m pa ka selebre viktwa defèt peyi m bèl jounen sila a.
Jounen retou Titid, jounen krisifiksyon jounen 1804.
Ban n peyi a ! Nou mande espas ! An n kontinye bale !

Seremoni banbòch yo se lasi nan je depevi byen mennen
Ki maske zo pouri deyè bèlte kadav simityè rekonsilyan
Nan yon chapèl malsite bèl pawòl malandren FMI ak BM
Ap koule nan zòrèy malere dezostobre, zonbi nan mayi
K'ap di Ayi Bobo pou wonga zòt malis, majisyen mal gadò !

Pa ban m sannanm ka Ozanfè pou chimen lespwa ;
Pèp la ap chache lavi avèk rèv li anvi. Vi vivan selebran.
Li pap pran kaka poul pou bè, ni levanjil pou lajan kontan.
Moun yo vle diyite ak respè ak vant plen. Yo vle trankilite.
Yo pa vle bèl jansiv, kakabè, fatra, malafwa pou lafwa !

Kraze zo n se vre men nou pa san santiman ;
Madichon kou magouy monnonk lòtbò dlo,
Plis malfetri putchis zenglendo ronronnaj
Nou kenbe la pi rèd, menmsi nou blayi tapi wouj
Pou marin meriken ka vin dodomeya doudouman !

Pèp vanyan pran libète l avèk fòs ponyèt pa l. Je klere.
Li pran l avèk rasin rezistans li li plante ak sakrifis
San koule l aseptc pou l konbat laterè laperèz sèvitid !
Fòk nou pa ranplase kout kouto asasen pa lapè simityè ;
Nou ka ankò kwè nan yon vi libere, ak solèy ak lanmè !

Menmsi kè m te kontan Kòk la te retounen,
Menmsi m te pataje lajwa pèp ginen lakay,
Mwen pat ka selebre defèt peyi an mwen
Nan yon viktwa Pyrrhus ki gen sant pwazon.
An n bale ! An n bale ! Chase tout vèmin sou tè a !

Dokiman biwokrat ranplase mechanste ogranjou,
Bèl pawòl ak priyè diskou bon santiman ranplase
Tout zaksyon pou moun vin tounen moun,
Moun k'ap dechifre mesaj sou tenèb san lojik.
Veye yo ! Veye yo ! Veyatif piyajè mizè pèp !

Kenbe fèm chè frè m ak chè sè m yo k akwoupi
Nan yon prizon lespri sou yon latè mazakwa ;
Kenbe la pa lage ! Demen n ap bwè dlo klè, kouwè
Je n ret louvwi, veyatif pou yon konsyans maltrete
Nan yon reyalite pyeje malfektè kou noumenm kreye.

Melodi rekonsilyasyon ant lèt ak sitwon
Nan yon kwelekwekwe banbòch ak kè mare
Sipòte pa monnonk plis benisman lepap
Se sèl konsekrasyon nan lamès bò lakay :
Veye yo ! Veye yo ! Siveye piyajè vandè mizè pèp !

Moun k'ap chache nanm yo
Pa kite teyat madigra lòlò je yo,
Yo ret toujou di non kont koze malvire ;
Non kont opresyon, dominasyon, okipasyon
Ideyal yo pa de twa fèy gate nan tout forè a !

Moun k'ap gade lwen ka wè anpil bagay ;
Y'ap toujou rete lib moun k'ap poze keksyon,
Moun ki ka navige nan lanmè move tan.
Wi n'ap libere yon jou ! Nou pèp lib vwayajè esperans :
N'ap reprann gouvènay lawoze. N'ap refè lanati danse !

(Boston, 15 oktòb 1994)

   In the Beast's Alley (Poems of conscience)

* Powèm sa a te pibliye premye fwa nan *Haïti-Progrès* an 1994. Li osijè entèvansyon « dan griyen » Etazini ann Ayiti ann oktòb 1994 pou reenstale Jan-Bètran Aristid sou pouvwa li te pèdi a apre koudeta militè 30 septanm 1991 lan.

The English version of this poem is: "The Water That We Drink and That Drawns"

Sa Pè Breda ta di*

*(dedye a Tousen Louvèti ann okazyon
komemorasyon 200 anivèsè sakrifis li)*

Li te sèmante sèt fwa
depi lavi pase sou tè zansèt Ginen
jiska kacho fè nwa Fò-di-Jou nan Jira
pase nan lakou bòfrè Napoleon mèt zafè
pou rasin libète ret donnen
menm sou chimen malakwa.

Pè Breda ta mande pou vanyan zile yo
remonte nan memwa depi tan vant mare
pou jwenn solisyon lagè malediksyon
kolon malveyan lage nan sen fanmi
pou simayen dezinyon deblozay.
Pè Breda ta renmen menm lè l pa ta la
pou ti zanj plantasyon vize wo
menm lè sousèzo vle diskòd
ant zòt yo k'ape chante lespwa.

Pè Breda pat kriye
menm lè l te santi li maljwe
nan mennen Hédouville
makonnen ak Rigaud tou de bò
pou twonke jou leve avèk lannwit tonbe
Pè Breda tap gen anpil lapenn
lè li wè pyetinman respè kou lajistis
nan rapò pèp ak pèp
e peyi ak peyi e peyi avèk pèp
paske sa pa tap fè monnonk Sam plezi.

Pè Breda ta mande
pou lanmò Dominique jwenn vanjans
pou yo lage Noriega avèk eskiz sadwa
pou moun manje vant plen Dimanch Pak
pou laviktwa jistis nan lanmò Sandino

   In the Beast's Alley (Poems of conscience)

pa trikaj rizezri ta vini yon epifani
pou afimasyon dwa moun
Pè Breda ta mande
pou peye reparasyon lanmò Tonton Chalmay
e pou desten lil lan depi de syèk lanfè Leclerc
te tabli anba kòd kraze-zo avèk fòs
vin tounen yon temwayaj laglwa
banbou yo ap pliye men ki pa vle kase.

Pè Breda ta mande
pou Irak pa vin sen ni pretèks
ni pou viktim mize libreri bonbade
ki mouri anba lapli misil ann Arabi
pa tounen pyon laglwa onorab enperyal.

Nan kacho nan Jira
Pè Breda te jire pou zetwal li plase
nan konstelasyon nan kwen nwa
pou blayi reyonnman libète
li te sèmante pou sa ki te pase
pa t retounen pou kwafe delivrans
—Pè Breda tap mande pou lapè reye.

Sa pè Breda ta di
si l ta wè de san zan
pat pote yon oazis laplenn fleri
nan kè malediksyon plantasyon ?
Sa l ta di si solèy pat leve
si komin Kapwa ta vin detwi
sa l ta di si wosiyòl pat chante jou maten ?

Sa Pè Breda ta di
si nou pèdi lespwa ?
Sa l ta di si sa yo ki sove nan zile
retounen memwa yo resplandi
pou bati Ayiti ?

Sa Pè Breda ta di
si maswife pat grenpe premye janvye ?
si bazilik pat konn kwape chanm ante ?
si Antwann nan Gome te sèl pap ?
sa l ta di si l wè moun pedevi
pote flè bay anvayisè ansòselè
sou plas Baghdad an plen nè CNN ?

Sa Pè Breda ta di si l santi l
pèp fache jwenn ak Bonapat dekalke
pou dekonstwi tout sa k te la
sa l ta di devan poud nan je
medya sou koudjyak ap lwanje.

Kouman Pè Breda ta santi l
lè li wè Pòtoprens fin dekonstonbre
anba eksplozyon chay kretyenvivan
k ap kouri anba lonb sosyal pèdisyon
sa Pè Breda ta di si nou pa ret anvi
pou kontinye reve
pou yon lòt jounen louvwi ?

* The English version of this poem is: "What Would Old
Breda Say"

    In the Beast's Alley (Poems of conscience)

Òd dlo nan je pou Gaza

Apre tout misil vin voye
apre wout koupe an de
nan chimen san rive
apre alam sirèn anbilans
ap sonnen san rete
pou kanale estwopye lopital
e silans tabli kou yon move sò
apre katye depalaw
mi kay ki tounen sann
zo ki jete nan fòs komin
menm chen pa ka jwenn dlo pou bwè.

Apre lopital pa gen plas
apre mòg yo ranpli
sakristen pa gen chan
plant yo pa ka leve
sou tab pa gen diri
manje sèlman sèvi
lè lachans fè oun ti souri.

Apre lekòl fèmen
san yo pa di pèsonn
apre oun fanmi pèdi frè e sè
papa ak manman ak kouzen
ak zanmi bò lakay
apre san fin tounen pou latè
senp eleman koulan pou piyay.

Apre pa gen kote pou kouri
e menm lakay vin tounen kalvè
e sib pou bal tijènjan nan lame Izrayèl
apre rele timoun nan grangou
zo yo kale kou jibye ka bouche.

Apre w anvayi tè nou
jete bonb sou tout kretyevivan

kouwè myèt bisuit pou pijon
apre ou detwi lavi nou
tire bal sou menm sekou ijans
fèmen mache anba tout lavil
kreye rivyè koule ak san lapenn
detwi tout biwo batistè e brile
tout kote lannwit nou konn flannen.

Apre ou fè tout sa w vle
pou yo pa ta janm ekziste
apre w itilize tout zam
pou bare tout vwa ki di non
ou rete toujou yon tèt kre kou yon kwi
toujou makonnen nan move nanm ou
toujou petri sou pwa laperèz
toujou menase pa global angloutisman
toujou anpetre nan tèt chaje.

Apre ou fin fè e defè
pou vanje nan memwa w
depòtasyon ak ekzil
chanm a gaz ak kè mare
zansèt ou te andire
nou ka jwenn nan memwa latè
e pataje ansanm plizyè milenè
dlo nan je ak rèv pou lavi
ankenn nou pa gen monopòl malsite
ankenn nou pa sèl manm Linivè.

Menm apre plizyè dekad tribilasyon
Gaza toujou ret anvi ap goumen
Gaza pa reskonsab pou move sò w
se pwòp ou ki kreye lanfè pa w.

Gaza se pa Hamas
men Hamas sot nan matris Gaza
vote pou gouvènman oun moun vle
èske se pa sa yo di demokrasi ye ?

    In the Beast's Alley (Poems of conscience)

Vote pou gouvènman oun moun vle
pa vle di sèlman si gwo peyi apwouve.
Kote k pa gen jistis pa ka gen lapè
nou tout se timoun yo bliye
k'ap suiv konpa pakou latè je fèmen
tout masak se masak
ke l rive nan Gaza ou nan Qana
nan Ramallah, Haditha oubyen nan Haifa
ke l rive nan Fallujah
nan World Trade Center
oubyen nan Site Solèy.

Gaza se pa Hamas
men nou tout se Gazayen
konsyans ki pa donte k'ap lite
pou dwa pou yon demen miyò
dwa pou nou deside sa nou vle.

Izrayèl koze lanmò san bezwen
sa se laverite desandelye piknik
menmsi Gaza pa Nouyòk ni Filadèlfi
ni Wachintonn DC ni Boston
san k koule frape pòt konsyans nou tout.

Tiye yon mas moun nan kèlke zè
se krim lagè nan Auschwitz
kouwè nan Guernika
oubyen nan Srebrenica kòm nan Gaza
chanjman se sispann defannn san rezonnman
avèk zye kale yo tòtire
tout malsite Izrayèl
chanjman se mande pou sa chanje.

Gaza se peche nou tout anndan kè n
konsyans ak memwa istwa latè
memwa malsite ki pat dwe rive
memwa jistis ki dwe blayi
konsyans pou Gaza libere.

Doulè dwe reyini olye li divize
istwa ak memwa mechanste
olye se obstak gran chimen
fè pase pou laperèz simayen
dwe lanse tout vag yo
nan zèv levasyon pou tout limanite
nou dwe kriye pèt tout sa k ale yo
an n pran randevou sou wout nouvo lespwa.

(Boston, janvye 2009)

* The English version of this poem is: "Od of Tears for Gaza"

In the Beast's Alley (Poems of conscience)

Onè-respè pou timoun yo!

(dedye a tout tibebe ki fèk fèt)

Vini timoun, vini!
lonè-respè pou ou,
nou swete w byenveni
avèk bwa nou louvri
pou n akeyi nanm ou
sou yon solèy fè frèt
anba yon lapli san dlo
sou yon tè san manje!

Vini timoun, vini!
vin ede nan konbit
vin bay bra ak lajwa
nan lakou marasa!
Vin pote tanbou lou
nan dans Gede Nibo!
Vini timoun vini!
vin fè lavi fleri
sou yon tè san souri!

    (1995)

* The English version of this poem is: "Welcome to the Children"

Haitian Creole (Kreyòl Ayisyen)

Haitian Creole is spoken by about 10.5 million people in Haiti and 4 million outside Haiti (mostly in the United States, Canada, France, and other Caribbean and Latin American countries such as Dominican Republic, Cuba, Bahamas, French Guiana, Ivory Coast, Guadeloupe, Martinique, Trinidad and Tobago, Venezuela, etc.).

The syntax or structure of the language is derived from West African languages such as Wolof, Fon and Ewe. The vocabulary is largely French-based, with influences from English and Spanish. Haitian Creole is one of Haiti's two official languages (the other one is French). The Haitian Creole's pronunciation is phonetic. There are no silent letters.

The Alphabet of Haitian Creole

Consonants:
b, ch, d, f, g, h, j, k, l, m, n, ng, p, r, s, t, v, z

Vowels:
a, e, en, i, o, on, ou, u, ui, w, y,

Nasal vowels:
an, àn, è, en, ò

Consonant vowels:
w, wà, wò

All sounds are always spelled the same, except when a vowel carries a "grave accent." When a word is immediately followed by a vowel, the digraphs denoting the nasal vowels (*an*, *en*, *on*, and sometimes *oun*) are pronounced as an oral vowel followed by *n*.

   In the Beast's Alley (Poems of conscience)

Haitian Creole verbs are not inflected for tense or person, and there is no grammatical gender per se (adjectives and articles are not inflected according to the noun). Plural and possessive forms are indicated by markers like *yo, ou, m, w*. There are six pronouns, one pronoun for each person/number combination. There is no difference between direct and indirect pronoun.

> Mwen (first person singular / Short form, M)
> Ou (second person singular / Short form, W)
> Li (third person singular / Short form, L)
> Nou (first person plural / Short form, N)
> Ou or Nou (second person plural / Short form, W)
> Yo (third person plural / Short form, Y)

Possession is indicated by placing the possessor or possessive pronoun after the item possessed. There are two indefinite articles in Haitian Creole: *yon* or simply *on* or *oun* (ek. yon machin / a car).

There is also a definite article resembling the English *the* and French *le/la*. It is important to note that the definite articles are placed *after* the noun.

The Haitian Creole verbs remain the same and have one form, the tense or mood or context are indicated by markers (ap, te, pral, gen, etc.)

Bibliography and On-line Resources:

Degraff, Michel (2001). "Morphology in Creole genesis: Linguistics and ideology". In Kenstowicz, Michael. *Ken Hale: A life in language.* Cambridge: MIT Press. pp. 52–121Haitian Creole Language and Culture Summer Institute: http://www.umb.edu/academics/caps/summer_programs/institutes/haitiancreoleAnn Pale Kreyòl / Indiana University Creole Institute: http://indiana. edu/~creole/Fattier, Dominique (1998). "Contribution à l'étude de la genèse d'un créole: L'Atlas linguistique d'Haïti, cartes et commentaires (Dissertation)". *Language in Society* (Université de Provence)Lefebvre, Claire (1985) Relexification in creole genesis revisited: the case of Haitian Creole. In Muysken & Smith (eds.) *Substrate versus Universals in Creole Genesis*. Amsterdam: John Benjamins.

Kreyol.com: http://www.kreyol.com/dictionary.html

MIT Department of linguistics and philosophy: http://web .mit.edu/linguistics/people/faculty/degraff/publications .html

   In the Beast's Alley (Poems of conscience)

Glossary of non-English words used in the poems

Agwe, Agoe: Another Vodou god of the sea, and also of travel, exile.

Ayibobo: A greeting expression in the Haitian vodou rituals that means literally: "Hail to the spirits," an expression of welcome.

Bòkò: A sorcerer or a devilish houngan.

Champs-de-Mars: Memorial Park in Port-au-Prince, in honor of Haiti's independence heroes.

Cafard: Spleen. Sadness; feeling of profound desolation.

changer la vie: To change life, in the sense of making it better.

Chute libre: Free fall.

Commandeur: militarily-trained supervisor or discipline enforcer on the slave plantation.

Complétude: State of completeness, perfection of the thing in itself.

Dépravés: Corrupted; sexually debauched.

Entendement: Faculty to understand intellectually as opposed to sensation.

Gibiers: Flock. Animal farmed and used as food.

Gede Nibo: One of the Gede loas. Familiar name of Gede, the Vodou god of the deceased, but also of the libido, known for his foul language and sexual openness.

Goudougoudou: Earthquake. Neologism invented during the Haitian 2010 earthquake.

Griot: Literary movement in Haiti in the 1930s and 1940s. Sage, teacher, philosopher, memorialist for a specific locality or region.

Ginen: Referring to Africa, the Haitian ancestral home.

Houngan, Manbo: a Vodou priest.

Incomplétude: State of incompleteness, imperfection of the thing.

Hounsi, Ounsi: Initiated, important practicing member of Vodou in whose body the loa manifests him/herself.

Kòk: Rooster. Referring here to its representation as the symbol of Aristide's Lavalas movement.

Larrons en foire: Literally thieves in a fair.

Lasalin: A famous Port-au-Prince slum.

L'enfant terrible: Literally the terrible child. Used sometimes in the sense of someone with fierce temper or who engages in impulsive, dare-devil endeavors.

Lespri: Spirit. The word has a more mysterious and magical connotation in Haitian Creole.

Loa, Lwa: Spirit or "mystery" in the Vodou religion; he/she is considered as the messenger or the intermediate between God and humans.

Madrasa: School in Arabic.

Major-Jon, Majò-Jon: The biggest or the main jon in a Haitian rara band.

Makabral: Noun invented by the author, meaning personification of the macabre.

Maldyòk: Curse of bad luck (evil eye).

Maswife, Masuife: A game consisting of a pole made slippy with grease that one has to climb to win a prize. It used to take place on every January 1st in Haiti.

Nanm: is a Haitian word which means together soul, spirit, consciousness, sometimes with a more complex connotation meaning intelligence, clairvoyance, awareness and cognitive faculty. Often referred as the "essence" of an individual; the zonbi is the one who has lost that essence.

In the Beast's Alley (Poems of conscience)

Négrier: The name of the boats that transported the slaves from Africa to Haiti.

Oumfò: A Vodou sanctuary.

Oshun: Another name for Ogoun or Ogou.

Pécheresse: Sinner, feminine genre.

Potomitan: The main, central pole erected in the middle of a Vodou temple.

Rêverie: State of dreaming; day dreaming; existential idealization.

SEAL: Acronym for Sea, Air, and Land. Special force of the United States Navy.

Simbi: The Vodou god of sea, water, singing, who lives in deep water.

Simbi-nan-dlo: Meaning Simbi-in the-Water; in reference to Simbi.

Site Solèy: A famous Port-au-Prince slum.

Solèy, Soleil: Sun in Haitian Creole and in French.

Sursis: Momentary suspension. Temporary stay of execution.

Tchouboum: Trouble, serious problem, calamity

Unsoul: Word invented by the author, someone deprived of soul. The personificator of such a state.

Va-nus-pieds, Vanipye: Shoeless or Bare-footed. In venerable reference to the Haitian anti-slavery combatants who fought bare-footed the mighty forces of the French empire.

Vèvè: Ritual graphics or drawings to express welcoming disposition to the loa; they're usually placed on the floor of the *oumfò,* preferably around the *potomitan,* usually seen on the floor of the peristil (temple), sometimes on the wall.

Veye yo: Watch out for them.

Vodou: The Haitian religion or belief system.

Zombie, Zonbi, Zombi, Zonbification: A person presumably killed by a Vodou spell. The "dead" will be resurrected in a half-dead half-alive state of semi-consciousness which makes him/her malleable by the "bòkò" (a Vodou sorcerer) who had induced the "death." However, if the zonbi tastes salt, he/she will regain normal consciousness and, often, fight back. The inducement of the zonbi state.

In the Beast's Alley (Poems of conscience)

Profile of the author

Poet, critic and essayist, Tontongi (Eddy Toussaint) writes in Haitian, in French, and in English. His latest book is the trilingual collection of essays and poems *Poetica Agwe* (2012). Tontongi is the editor of the trilingual politico-literary journal *Tanbou*: (www.tanbou.com).

Other releases by Trilingual Press
Autres parutions chez Presse Trilingue
Lòt piblikasyon lakay Près Trileng

Georges Jean-Charles
Jacques Stéphen Alexis, romancier de Compère Général Soleil
[Essais 364 p. Mars 2013]

Patrick Sylvain
Masuife
[Koleksyon powèm, 100 p. Mas 2013]

Nicole Titus
Plato / Platon : Apology, Crito, Phaedo / Apoloji, Kriti, Fedo
[Translation/Tradiksyon, 100 p. Desanm/December 2012]

Dumafis Lafontan
Krik? Krak! Dèyè Mòn Gen Mòn / Mountains Behind Mountains
[Bilingual collection of poems, 134 p. Desanm/December 2012]

Frantz-Antoine Leconte
René Depestre: du chaos à la cohérence
Contributeurs : Robenson Bernard, Etienne Télémarque, Bernadette Carré Crosley, Eddy Magloire, Amy J. Ransom, Clément Mbom, Sarah Juliet Lauro, Cauvin Paul, Silvia U. Baage et Léon-François Hoffman.
[Anthologie d'essais, 354 pages, 2012]

   In the Beast's Alley (Poems of conscience)

Tontongi and Jill Netchinsky
The Anthology of Liberation Poetry
Contributors: Joselyn M. Almeida, Ali Al-Sabbagh, Marc Arena, Soul Brown, Richard Cambridge, Neil Callender, Berthony Dupont Martín Espada, L'Mercie Frazier Patricia Frisella, Regie O'Hare Gibson, Marc D. Goldfinger, Calvin Hicks, Gary Hicks, Jack Hirschman, Everett Hoagland, Paul Laraque, Daniel Laurent, Denizé Lauture, Danielle Legros Georges, Tony Medina, Jill Netchinsky-Toussaint, Tanya Pérez-Brennan, Thomas Phillips, Ashley Rose Salomon, Margie Shaheed, Cheo Jeffery Allen Solder, Patrick Sylvain, Aldo Tambellini, Tontongi, Askia M.Touré, Tony Menelik Van Der Meer, Frantz "Kiki" Wainwright, Brenda Walcott, Anna Wexler, and Richard Wilhelm. [Anthology of poems, 320 pages, January 2010]

Tontongi
Poetica Agwe
Essays, Poems and Testimonials on Resistance, Peace, and the Ideal of Being / Esè, powèm e temwayaj sou rezistans, lapè e ideyal nanm nou / Essais, poèmes et témoignages sur la résistance, la paix et l'idéal d'être
[A trilingual edition / Yon edisyon an twa lang / Une édition trilingue [420 p. 2011]

Dumas F. Lafontant
After the Dust Settles
[Bilingual collection of poems / Koleksyon powèm bileng (English-Ayisyen), 136 pages, Fall 2010]

Marie-Thérèse Labossière Thomas
Clerise of Haiti
[Novel, 378 pages, 2010]

Dr. Vinod A. Mittal

Low Back Pain And Low Back Care

An edition in five languages (English, Hindi, Spanish, Haitian, and Portuguese)

Contributors: Priti V. Mittal, Altagracia P. Mayers, Idi Jawarakim, Patricia B.P. Dos Santos.

[Medical advice on physical therapy, 82 pages, 2009]

Franck Laraque

Paul Laraque : Éclaireur de l'aube nouvelle

Contributeurs : Josaphat-Robert Large, Frantz-Antoine Leconte, Hughes St-Fort, Max Manigat, Frantz Latour, Jean Métellus, Jean Prophète, René Depestre, Robert Garoute, Gérard Pétrus, Claude Pierre, Elie Leblanc, Jr., Gary Klang, Karèn Bogat, Georges Jean Charles, Denizé Lauture, Clotaire Saint-Natus, Lochard Noël, Serge François, Berthony Dupont, Papados, Jean André Constant, Danielle Laraque Arena, Jack Hirschman, Michele Laraque, Marc Anthony Arena, Hatuey Laraque Two Elk, Ashley Laraque, Max Schwartz, Prosper Sylvain, Jr., Gabrielle Vimer, Anthony Phelps, Rodney Saint-Eloi, Gérard Etienne, Eddy Mésidor, Emmanuel Gilles, Frantz Ludeke, Fritz Clermont, Camille Gauthier, Kern Delince, Raymond Chassagne, Jean Gateau, Jean Claude Valbrun, Tontongi, Jean Mapou, Roger Savain, Michel-Ange Hyppolite. [Essais, 180 pages, été 2009]

Tontongi

Voices of the Sun: The Anthology of Haitian Writers Published in the Review Tanbou / Les Voix du Soleil: Anthologie des écrivains haïtiens publiés dans la revue Tanbou / Vwa Solèy pale: antoloji ekriven ayisyen pibliye nan revi Tanbou

        In the Beast's Alley (Poems of conscience)

Contributeurs/Kontribitè/Contributors: Paul Laraque, Tontongi (Eddy Toussaint), Hugues St.Fort, Papadòs (Fritz Dossous), Jean-André Constant, Berthony Dupont, Marc Arena, Doumafis Lafontan, Nounous (Lenous Surprice), Yvon Joseph, Patrick Louis, Edner Saint-Amour, Charlot Lucien, Emmanuel Védrine, André Fouad, Rodelaire Octavius, Janvier Lesly Junior, Bobby Paul, Jean Saint-Vil, Franck Laraque, Jack Hirschman, Lee Chance, Glodel Mezilas, Melissa Beauvery, Cathy Delaleu, Jean-Dany Joachim, Roberto Strongman, Guamacice Délice, Huguens Louis-Pierre, Vilvalex Calice, Elsie Suréna, Denise Bernhardt, Duccha (Duckens Charitable), Suzy Magloire-Sicard, Michel-Ange Hypopolite, Patrick Sylvain, Barbara Victome, Jeanie Bogart, Gary Daniel, Johnny Bélizaire, Denizé Lauture, Fred Edson Lafortune, Jamie Moon, Pierre-Roland Bain, Idi Jawarakim, Danielle Legros-Georges, Edwald Delva, Oreste Joseph, Serge-Claude Valmé, Doug Tanoury, Prosper "Makendal" Sylvain, Jr., Brian Sangudi, Anna Wexler, Marilène Phipps. Photos and paintings by / photos et peintures par / foto ak tablo pa: David Henry, Michel Doret, Don Gurewitz, Marilène Phipps, Blondèl Joseph. [Poèmes et essais trilingues and illustrations, 404 p. Septanm 2007]

Denizé Lauture
Madichon Sanba: Dlo nan Sensè a
[Koleksyon powèm, me 2003]

Tontongi with the Liberation Poetry Collective
Poets Against the Killing Fields
Contributors: Askia Touré, Aldo Tambellini, Brenda Walcott, Jill Netchinsky, Joselyn Almeida, Neil Calender, Tontongi, Anna Wexler, Gary Hicks and Tony Medina. [Anthology of poems, 170 pages, September 2007]

Paul Germain
Love and Other Poems by Haitian Youths
Contributors: Bernadin Bastien, Célemme Biennestin, Evens Ciméa, Erlia Dessin, Elie Fortuné, Paul E Germain, Samson Germain, Gustave Neslyn Josh, Judeline Jean Baptiste, Sandra Lamontagne, Remylus Losius, Rubens Maisonneuve, Mario Morency, Ruth Norvilus, Jonas Saint-Aubin, Emmanuel W. Védrine, Farah Paul, Wilguens Sainterling, Ebed Sainterling, Gems Dorvil, Charles Jean-Baptiste, Fabrice Mont-Louis. [Trilingual anthology of poems, 80 pages, July 2004]

    In the Beast's Alley (Poems of conscience)

Books in preparation
Livres en préparation
Liv k'ap prepare (2013)

Charlot Lucien
La tentation de l'autre rive / Tantasyon latravèse
[Poèmes bilingues (français-ayisyen), 90 p. Otònn /
Automne 2013]

Edwald Delva
Adelina
[Woman, 200 p. Otònn 2013]

Tontongi
Memwa Baboukèt / La Gueule du Trublion
[Essais bilingues (français-ayisyen), 240 p. Prentan /
Printemps 2014]

Franck Laraque
L'instrumentalisation de la pensée révolutionnaire
[Essais en trois langues, 544 p. Ete/Été/Summer 2013]

Cheo Jeffery Allen Solder
One4deBrovahs
[Essays, memoir, 150 p. Automn 2013]

Trilingual Press
trilingualpress@tanbou.com
http://tanbou.com/trilingualpress/index.htm

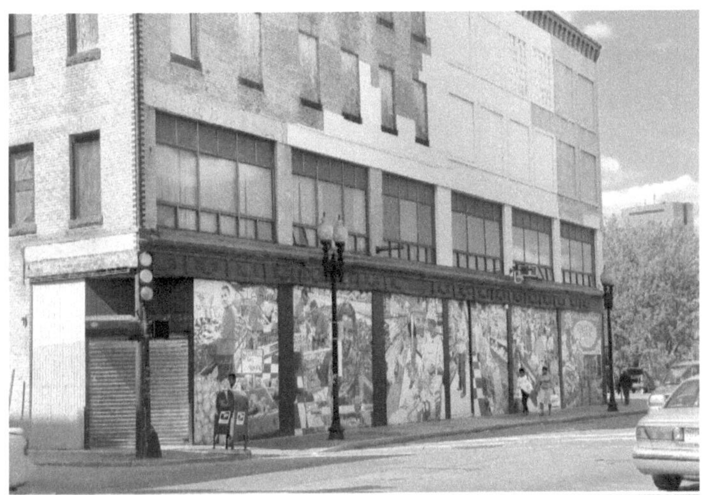

A view of the corners of Washington Street and Melnea Cass Boulevard, in Roxbury, Boston —*photo by Patrick Sylvain, 2013.*